MW00636956

"Matt explores the intimate and dynamic relationship of Fatherhood and Sonship. In Matthew 13 as Jesus is talking about the four types of soil, have you ever wondered why He talks about the 100, 60, and 30-fold life? *A King's Fire* is a vulnerable and articulate journey into practicing Christianity. If you are "good soil" and want to explore the 100-fold life of intimacy with the Father, read this book."

—AAMON ROSS
Founder & President of Kingdom In Politics
www.kingdominpolitics.com
www.join.kingdominpolitics.com

"It's time for kings to wake-up and walk in a way that is uncompromising and passionate about seeing His Kingdom come on earth as it is in heaven, to the end. This book will inspire you to live a life that is fully 'sold-out' for Jesus - The King of kings. The time is now!"

—RICHARD L JELFS
President, North America & Canada Charnwood, Inc.

"For over a decade, Matt and I served together in ministry. His passion for Jesus, his family, and living an authentic Spirit-filled life, has always been his highest priority. All that passion has been poured out of his heart and into *A King's Fire*. His successes and his failures have all served to help form a vision that will hopefully ignite your passion. In this book, you will find encouragement and instruction to help you step into the identity you were always meant to have."

—STEVE HEEREMA
Senior Pastor
Newton Church of the Way

"Every Monday, early in the morning, Matt, myself and a few other kings meet to share our hearts and pray. We watch the sunrise over the Sacramento River and each week are reminded of God's goodness in our lives. I have the pleasure of walking alongside this king. I get to hear his story, see his heart, know his process. He brings me courage, hope and the strength I need to throw off everything that hinders. Through the pages of *A King's Fire* I hear this familiar kind and challenging voice that calls me to more. It's a voice I treasure in my life and I know this book will be one that your treasure too."

—DAVE HILL

Bethel Children's Ministry Director
& Founder of HeartSmart TV

"In the book of Revelation, one of the first truths God reveals to the church is this: Jesus "has made us ***kings*** and ***priests*** to His God and Father." (Revelation 1:6) This royalty and priesthood of believers has often been lost in the religiosity of much of Christendom. In *A King's Fire,* Matt calls us back to the truth ***and*** the experience of this powerful revelation. Jesus is the King of kings. The kings that He reigns over includes not only the kings of the nations, but every one of us as His sons and daughters. We have been rescued from the Kingdom of darkness and been brought into the Kingdom of God, not just to be servants, but to be His sons and daughters. And that makes us royalty! The blood of a King runs in our veins. He has "made us kings." We are seated with Christ NOW on a heavenly throne and have been given the incredible privilege and destiny to usher that Kingdom into this present world, until "the kingdoms of this world become the kingdoms of our Lord and of His Christ, and He shall reign forever and ever." (Revelation 11:15) Using powerful testimonies from his own life to open up Biblical revelation, Matt beckons us to enter into that Kingdom realm and live in the reality of the King's fire! Having known Matt and his family personally, I can endorse not only this book but the man. Matt lives what he preaches, carrying a king's fire wherever he goes! "

—JOHN TAYLOR

Bethel Redding Missions Pastor

"Matt shares deeply from a marriage of experience with deep faith and trust. In the time I've known Matt, I've observed him living through some of the most challenging times in business and life. He has made the choice to to excel in it. Much of which he has shared about in *A King's Fire*. His focus rings true that God desires to prepare men and women to step into all He planned for them. Often, this involves purifying fire. Perhaps unpleasant but essential to be the gold that the Father sees in us. Matt gives hope and guidance along life's journey for those choosing to travel the road, and desiring to step into much more than the mundane. I encourage you to step forward and take the plunge too. Be blessed!"

—KEITH LEMMER
Inventor, Engineer

"I'm glad this book is finally out of this man. Matt is an amazing man who is after God's own heart. I've witnessed him say yes to Jesus over and over again even as he goes through the fire of refinement. His life stories will inspire you to say yes in a similar manner that will attract the voice of God as well as the deeds of God in your life."

—KOBINA ABBAN-SAAH
Friend and fellow king

"Matthew Hugg takes his readers on a powerful, courageous and compelling journey of becoming. Be aware it is written by a world changer and it is meant for world changers!"

—EDGAR SAVAGE BROWN
CEO of Rockstars Solar

"This book puts words to things I already believe and confirms so many things I feel God is doing in this time in history. The topics unpacked in this book will reshape your thoughts and your approach to life."

—TREY BOLLINGER
Owner, Lifetime Hunts

IT'S TIME TO IGNITE

A KING'S FIRE

MATTHEW HUGG

A King's Fire

Cover Design by Matthew Hugg
Interior Layout by BookBloks.com
Author Photo by Jessica Hugg

Hardcover ISBN: 978-1-7350882-5-9
Paperback ISBN: 978-1-7350882-6-6
eBook ISBN: 978-1-7350882-7-3

Printed in the United States of America

TABLE OF CONTENTS

INTRODUCTION

I'm writing this book because I've never read a book like this, and yet in my Spirit, I've always wanted to hear someone say these things... to articulate a path to kingship with the voice and tone a Father would use to admonish and encourage a son. The path to kingship is an invitation to hold in tension our fierce warrior spirit that is always up for the fight and the intimate connection we share with our Abba Father, our Commander, the King of Kings. As I've explored the path for myself, I've had so many questions. When do you pick up a sword and when do you worship? Are those things really that different? Who informs our assignments and how do we access true supernatural power and not simply default to our skills and talents? When is a dream too big? When do you go into the wilderness and when should you just take the common sense path? How do we endure well? How do you wield great power in Christ but maintain self-control and grace for yourself and others? How do we remain surrendered to His love and not get lured off track by temptations, circumstances, and our enemy?

In my ongoing prayer for guidance, I have been blessed with the best mentor anyone could ask for, and Holy Spirit has filled the role with the kindness, patience, and grace that no other human ever could.

I'm forever His grateful and humble student and friend. Along the way, He's given me many spiritual fathers and mentors to speak into my life and I'm grateful for them as well. Many of the lessons learned in this book come from them.

While I've sat under some outstanding leaders and have led many teams both in church and business, I confess I may be the least qualified author you've ever read. I write more from a place of desire and discovery as one immersed in the journey and not because of my credentials or accomplishments. I'm not an expert in kingship, nor do I possess an impressive resume or pedigree worthy of your time or attention. But if you think about it, that may be precisely the point behind Holy Spirit's commissioning me to write this. Perhaps you can see yourself in my "ordinary" journey to discover our extraordinary destiny as a beloved son of the King of Kings.

To be clear, this is not a Christian self-help, "5 easy steps" sort of book. There is no quick formula to manifesting your inner King that I'm aware of and no two paths are the same. Your journey to kingship with our Father is unique and the ways He has trained me may or may not apply in your life.

I am, however, certain of one thing. In the coming pages, Holy Spirit will ignite a fire in your gut that will call you into something new and greater than you can imagine. My prayer is that in the stories of my victories, failures, my hunger to know him, and my desire to know myself, you'll discover who your Father really is, and Holy Spirit will kindle a fierce desire to lay claim to your royal identity, role, and territory that He has given you.

Let me start by validating your journey.

Whatever path has led you here, I honor you as a brother and fellow king in the making. If you're a young David faithfully tending sheep in the wilderness and praising God while no one is watching or if you're a Caleb, the elder who still wants to fight a few giants before the end - you're welcome here. If you're rich or poor; if you're a busy family man, a businessman, a politician, a pastor of a small flock or a preacher to thousands - I honor you.

For those of you who have stood your post faithfully, who have run a powerful race, and who are ready for the next assignment - I'm thrilled to run with you.

For those who feel disqualified because you've lost some big fights - thank you for coming back to the altar. For those whose ministries or marriages have failed, or who've battled addictions, bankruptcies, or broken relationships - I honor your sacrifices, your challenges, and I'm glad you're here.

For those who feel discouraged, defeated, and disqualified - listen to the voice of your Heavenly Father and King speak words of truth and life over you. You're not disqualified. You're not damaged goods. You're not destined to sit on the sidelines of your own life because of your failures - past, present, or future.

You are a part of a royal family and the Earth is desperately waiting for you to shake off the dust and go another round. I recall one of my spiritual fathers and fellow king, Kevin, speaking these words over me one specific Sunday morning in the wake of my failure. From this point forward, I declare Romans 8:1 over you that says:

> *Romans 8:1 (NLT): So now there is no condemnation for those who belong to Christ Jesus.*

By the authority we have through Jesus to be ministers of His grace, and as your brother in arms, I declare that while you read this book; you are free from condemnation and I cancel the assignment and arrest the attacks of shame, doubt, fear, and all other attacks from your spiritual enemies, from people around you, or even from yourself. They have no hold on you as we spend this time together. Your mind and spirit are free to be renewed, dream again, to come alive.

We agree together to resist the temptation to give air-time to our past failures, or rant about systems or people that wounded us. We abandon the strategies, methods, and talents that we've learned to rely on for our own success and the pride that undermines our victories. With the wisdom of Heaven, we make peace with all of it, both the victories and the failures, and lean into a relationship with our King where he will give us insight to make sense of all of it. We partner with Holy Spirit to turn our ash heaps into beautiful monuments of victory to His Glory. By faith, we step into our training so that He can show us how to turn immovable mountains into smooth roads and take down even the biggest giants. In Jesus' name, Amen.

Now that we've aligned our mindsets with the truth of Heaven, let me tell you where we're going.

I'm an external processor, a curious observer, a hopeless idealist and passionate warrior poet that loves a good story. I'm writing this as a memoir to kings who have a desire to discover what is possible in this wild Kingdom we've inherited. Those imperfect but hungry sons who want to take responsibility for their journey, with a genuine desire to obey our King of Kings and to govern well the territory, treasure, time, and talents He's given them. In this book we'll meander through some of my personal experiences and unpack scripture as we let Holy Spirit reveal the nature of a true king who follows the King of Kings.

I've discovered that, for me, this journey had an important hinge point. This hinge was the moment I transitioned out of the shallow end of the religion "pool" where I was driven by the power of "should" and out into the deep waters of desire to be with my Father, to come alive in His Kingdom, and to discover who I was - at any cost.

Sadly, I admit there was, and sometimes still is, a strong temptation to linger in the shallows where the risks are low, the demands are not that great, and my own skills and abilities are enough. In the shallows, I "should" on myself when I mess up and accept the judgment of peers and guardians of the "rule book" as they "should" on me as well. While I may not struggle with any seriously destructive sin in the shallows, the subtle, slow violence of the shallows is that it's the place where I can get "frog boiled" without even knowing it as I focus on unimportant doctrines, traditions, and external appearances rather than internal transformation and the Holy Spirit's work.

In the shallows, a religious spirit encourages me to get comfortable while he slowly massages my mind with complacency and feeds me with partial truth that sounds good to my "itching ears".* In the shallows, it's acceptable to nurse a hidden grudge with the person I sit next to in church rather than seek reconciliation. It's expected that I'll hide my addictions to avoid judgment instead of receiving grace in an authentic community. In the shallows, a religious spirit tempts us with unhealthy vices to cope with the discouragement and disappointments of life. He robs my joy, my peace, and dulls the wonder of my new life in Christ. If I linger here unaware of his influence, my relationship with my King and my experience of His amazing Kingdom can slowly fade into the background as judgment, fear, anger, self-righteousness, religion, politics, and a host of other demons eventually consume me. Perhaps I'm not the only one?

But I'm filled with hope as I consider the question, "What if...?".

What if there is a place of such intense peace and joy reserved for me that my outer life could be an authentic reflection of my inner reality and not just an act?

What if I can calm storms and kill giants in my life, and teach my children and grandchildren to do the same?

What if I could change the atmosphere in the room from despair to hope just by showing up because Holy Spirit's presence in me is tangible?

What if the approval and affirmation of people had no power over me, but I was free to pursue my divine assignment without hesitation or reservation?

* Reference to 2 Timothy 4:3

What if instead of insulating my life from pain out of fear, I could learn to love the fire of refinement and view every trial as a stepping stone into a promotion of authority, wisdom, strength, and intimacy with Holy Spirit?

What if the supernatural was just my "natural" state?

What if I could generously administer the unlimited resources of Heaven into my family relationships, my business, city, church, school, and every other area of my life?

Could this be real? Isn't this what Jesus achieved for us when he died, rose from the dead, and was seated in heaven with all authority, dominion, and power?

I'm "all in" to discover this life and walk in divine destiny as a humble servant of the King of Kings, who has given us the keys to heaven and earth. I want to know the audacious depths of God's goodness as I carry out my assignment to be an ambassador from the Kingdom of Heaven to Earth.

I see Holy Spirit breathing on a smoldering fire that is burning away the "fleshiness" of a faith that has stalled out in the shallows of religion. He's revealing the pure-hearted warrior kings who are not particularly concerned with good behavior as defined by the Christian traditions or denominations from where they came. They're not distracted by past failures or by preserving their own comfort. Their faith is genuine, tested, relational, and driven by desire. They are loyal to one King.

This book is a rally cry for kings to jump out of the boiling pot and into their divine identity before it's too late. In it we'll learn the landscape of this new Kingdom we get to explore, learn to recognize the traps, and understand how to fight the good fight, and win. At its core, this book explores the central and most important discipline we are given in the new covenant - abiding - as Jesus describes in John 15:4.

I sense such a need for kings to arise as fathers and not just teachers and guides. Men who and speak life over a generation of spiritual orphans, stuck in the shallows, trying to prove themselves through performance and good behavior. In the shallows, we've developed skills and strategies that look good, but we've lost intimacy and wonder. We know how to build social media fan clubs and discipleship programs, but do we know how to abide? Do we know how to impart and initiate a young king into the Kingdom, or do we just volley information at them from a distance? We know theories and principles, but have our strategies and weapons ever been tested in battle?

This shift from teachers and guides to fathers is important for many reasons. Paul writes in 1 Corinthians:

> *1 Corinthians 4:15–21 (AMP): 15 After all, though you should have ten thousand teachers (guides to direct you) in Christ, yet you do not have many fathers. For I became your father in Christ Jesus through the glad tidings (the Gospel).*
>
> *16 So I urge and implore you, be imitators of me.*
>
> *17 For this very cause I sent to you Timothy, who is my beloved and trustworthy child in the Lord, who will recall to your minds my methods of proceeding and course of conduct and way of life in Christ, such as I teach everywhere in each of the churches.*
>
> *18 Some of you have become conceited and arrogant and pretentious, counting on my not coming to you.*
>
> *19 But I will come to you [and] shortly, if the Lord is willing, and then I will perceive and understand not what the talk of these puffed up and arrogant spirits amount to, but their force (the moral power and excellence of soul they really possess).*
>
> *20 For the kingdom of God consists of and is based on not talk but power (moral power and excellence of soul).*
>
> *21 Now which do you prefer? Shall I come to you with a rod of correction, or with love and in a spirit of gentleness?*

In the above passage, Paul calls out the arrogance and ineffectiveness of the teachers and guides attempting to lead the church in Corinth. He sent Timothy to show them the distinct difference between students who've received the gospel of "should", and spiritual sons who've received true, anointed impartation of power and revelation from their spiritual father.

I'd suggest we're at a similar point in Church history. We have pastors who'd rather pontificate than adopt spiritual sons and make true disciples. There is little to no loyalty or covenant among our spiritual family, but there is a lot of "church shopping". Unfortunately, many church cultures look more like a buffet of "take it or leave it" spiritual self-help with little relational connection between members rather than a spiritual family where mothers and fathers relationally raise and empower the next generation of Kingdom builders. If you're curious where you, or your church leaders, fall on this spectrum between teacher/guide vs. father, I've outlined a few distinct differences between teachers and fathers below.

- When you hear a Father speak, you feel you can kill giants. When you hear from a teacher, you feel you need to try harder and do better.
- Teachers want their students to embrace performance according to an external standard of behavior while fathers seek inward transformation and value obedience to Holy Spirit for their sons and daughters above all.
- Teachers make relatively low investment in relationships and coach their students on WHAT to think and how to behave. They value compliance and fill you with information until you agree with them. They take great care to gain credentials and take little responsibility for conversions, healthy relational connections, or tangible Kingdom impact.

- Fathers are invested for the long haul. They live life with you, like Jesus modeled with his disciples, and teach you HOW to think and remain connected relationally, even if we don't always agree.
- You're not a project to a father, you're a son. They won't abandon or shame you, even when you wound them, walk away from them, and make mistakes.
- Teachers warn you to avoid spiritual danger and play it safe.
- Fathers throw you in the deep end, stay close, and encourage you to learn to swim. Fathers are not afraid to have their sons put into storms, give them grace to flail as they learn, and celebrate them when they are victorious.

WHEN YOU HEAR A FATHER SPEAK, YOU FEEL YOU CAN KILL GIANTS. WHEN YOU HEAR FROM A TEACHER, YOU FEEL YOU NEED TO TRY HARDER AND DO BETTER.

- Fathers teach you to wait on God for instructions and endure. They value hunger and zeal for God and have the discipline to say No to a thousand "good" ideas because they only want the "God" idea. They don't want to create Ishmael's, they want to wait for the promised Isaac.
- Teachers promote formulas and structure that stress skill sets over anointing and control over obedience to the Holy Spirit. They are fearful of the unpredictability and vulnerability required to follow Holy Spirit.

Over time, I've noticed common qualities and characteristics I see in real kings. But the most important one that defines them all is this; they stay in love with their King of Kings. Nothing can defeat love. Nothing is better than love, nothing is more precious than love. When we stay in love, we steel ourselves against temptation. Kings who know how much they're loved know that they have received all things in Christ. That's why you can trust a real king. Everyone has a "price" except for a king who is fully known and loved by his Heavenly Father, the King of Kings. They are unstoppable, immovable, enforcers of the King's agenda to rescue and restore the Earth. It is their pleasure and joy to fight arm in arm with brothers to see His Kingdom come, on Earth as it is in Heaven, to the end.

Conversely, if a king falls out of love with the King of Kings, he'll fall into fear, boredom, or worse. They are compromisers, weak, and always negotiating for their lives, rather than losing it for their King. Jesus describes the scene pretty well.

> *Matthew 24:7–14 (NLT): Nation will go to war against nation, and kingdom against kingdom. There will be famines and earthquakes in many parts of the world. 8 But all this is only the first of the birth pains, with more to come.*
>
> *9 "Then you will be arrested, persecuted, and killed. You will be hated all over the world because you are my followers. 10 And many will turn away from me and betray and hate each other. 11 And many false prophets will appear and will deceive many people. 12 Sin will be rampant everywhere, and the love of many will grow cold. 13 But the one who endures to the end will be saved. 14 And the Good News about the Kingdom will be preached throughout the whole world, so that all nations will hear it; and then the end will come.*

Jesus says in the last days that our love will grow cold and we'll adopt a deceptive form of religion, but it will be powerless. A powerless, loveless king can't lead, can't inspire anyone, can't conquer any enemy or take territory. A powerless king whose love has grown cold runs away from giants. If this is you, receive this hope. Love reconnects us to the source of all power, revives a cold heart, and is the fuel that renews our courage to run into battle.

I want to inspire a generation of my contemporaries to be mighty men, champions, and spiritual operatives who carry out their royal assignments, honor their King and build His Kingdom - nothing more - nothing less. Kings who know the simple, sweet, discipline of abiding and won't trade intimacy for Earthly promotion. Kings who are not distracted by praise, nor criticism. Who place little value in either failure or success from man's perspective, but guard their connection to the King at all costs because they know apart from Him they can do nothing.

These are the ones God trusts to carry the weight of his glory and His mantle of authority on the Earth and in His Kingdom. They are truck drivers and farmers like my dad and bankers like my father-in-law. They are pastors and preachers and men I've walked with from the time I was young up to this very day like Keith, Bill, Kevin, Roger, Jason, Charlie, Bob, Mike, Andrew, Steve, Jonathan, IBen, Tim, Mark, Dave, Richard, Nick, Matt, Sam, Jeremy, Eddie, Aamon, Kobina, Alan, Johnny, and many others. They are entrepreneurs, teachers, chemists, nurses, soldiers, factory workers, politicians, evangelists, marketers, missionaries, programmers, inventors, craftsmen, and actors. And every one of them is a king, serving the King of Kings, faithfully standing their post, holding back the tide of evil attempting to consume our world today.

KINGS ARE UNSTOPPABLE, IMMOVABLE, ENFORCERS OF THE KING'S AGENDA TO RESCUE AND RESTORE THE EARTH.

They don't sweat their past failures or defeats. They don't live under the cloud of shame and regret. They lean into the promise that God restores the years the locusts have eaten and they regularly return to the altar to offer themselves as living sacrifices. They know how to set captives free. Whether governing nations or collecting garbage, they know it's all holy, sanctified work and they do it with our King's fire running through their veins.

The journey starts now. If a few people would like to come along, then I'd welcome the company. The road isn't always going to be smooth. This isn't a neutered and sanitized version of faith designed to appeal to those who've grown comfortable in the shallows.

For kings who've seen battle up close... for those who've known the rush of overwhelming victory, and can still taste blood in their mouth from crushing defeat... for the humble and hungry mighty men of God who run out to face their giants with a resolute and defiant grin as they relish the coming victory; I honor you and am eager to run with you. If the journey has taught me anything, it is that this is a marathon, not a sprint, but I've also discovered over and over again that it's worth every mile.

Chapter 1

DELIVERANCE

I remember the day vividly. It was a beautiful Fall day in a small Midwest city in the dead center of "flyover" country. I was headed to a meeting with Andrew, one of my spiritual mentors at church, as a part of a ministry leadership class my wife and I were taking. We were nearing the end of the meeting and he stopped, somewhat awkwardly, and told me he wanted to get a few other people to come in and pray with us and I agreed.

To be honest, I was pretty disengaged that day. Because of some frustrating and painful situations with a few close friends and a family member, I came in feeling pretty numb and my mentor could sense that I wasn't "feeling it" on this particular day. When he returned, he was accompanied by two more people, and the woman on his right immediately began praying loudly in tongues.

I had never heard anyone pray in tongues before and so I looked at her in confusion and asked her to repeat herself as if I hadn't understood her "greeting". The man on his left came in quietly and just put his hand on my shoulder and before I realized what was happening, I doubled over in agony. Like a spiritual ninja, he quickly jerked the table out from in front of me, so I didn't slam my head as I lurched forward. I involuntarily dove out of my chair and began writhing on the ground. Every muscle in my body was firing at 110% and I couldn't release them. It was like my body was crushing itself. I felt a vile rage consume me and a pure hatred for the people praying for me I couldn't explain. These are people I loved and had connected with over many years of relationship through college and after, but suddenly, I thrashed at them attempting to punch, kick and bite them. Along with this fury came a superhuman strength and I grappled on the ground, knocking over chairs, clawing and grabbing for them. Had any of my blows landed, I'm certain I would have injured them badly, but despite my thrashing, they somehow moved and dodged away from my attacks like Neo dodging bullets in the Matrix, yet they never took their hands off me and never stopped praying.

I HAD NEVER HEARD ANYONE PRAY IN TONGUES BEFORE AND SO I LOOKED AT HER IN CONFUSION AND ASKED HER TO REPEAT HERSELF AS IF I HADN'T UNDERSTOOD HER "GREETING".

As I screamed and sobbed, years of pain erupted to the surface as the demonic power of Bitterness and Anger succumbed to the power of Jesus' blood and the authority of these holy ministers of God's Kingdom. The physical pain was so intense I thought I was going to die of a brain aneurysm or heart attack. I heard in my head the demons say, "We'll leave, but we're going to kill you in the process."

This scene went on for a few minutes until I lay still on the ground, physically exhausted in a pool of my own tears and snot. I could barely open my eyes or lift myself from the floor. I could tell that I'd torn muscles in my legs, shoulders, arms, and stomach. As I painfully pulled myself up with their help, I looked up at these mentors in shock and bewilderment and simply asked one question, "What just happened?"

In my spirit, I think I knew what had happened, but my mind had no language or grid for understanding the event. These kinds of things were not readily discussed or taught about in the conservative evangelical church circles I grew up in. These precious ministers looked back into my face and their own looks of shock appeared and they told me I should go look in a mirror. I shuffled down the short hallway to the men's room and looked in the mirror to discover tiny streams of blood were appearing on my face over newly formed "freckles" and bruises, the result of crushing and straining so hard that I'd broken small capillaries in my face.

As I stood in the men's restroom, I felt my strength return. My muscles felt like they were being washed with a cool healing water and a sense of peace came over my mind and body. For the first time in my life, I wasn't angry. I wasn't angry.

I had never known what it felt like NOT to be angry! A fresh wave of tears and emotions rose in me, this time tears of joy and thankfulness. I kept thinking, "What just happened?"

Bitterness and Anger are demons. They are quickly attracted to specific events in our life, painful moments, moments of failure, moments where we are victimized by evil. Their job is to "help" you to interpret that event, and all following events of your life through their lenses of pain, criticism, judgment, and suspicion. They come in through your mind's intellectual gate after you've been wronged and provide you with an all-you-can-eat buffet of unhealthy thoughts designed to feed your wounds instead of heal them. They'll help you speculate about people's motives and intentions. They'll promote an inner monologue that makes you the victim and encourages you to nurse a grudge. They'll help you role play arguments over and over in your mind where you verbally thrash your adversary and reinforce your hatred for them.

They are liars, and every lie they whisper in your ear is designed to trap you in their prison. They will steal your joy, take you out of your destiny, and destroy your mental health, physical health, and your relationships. They'll even kill you if you let them.

By God's grace, He used two kings and one queen to drive them out of my life on what turned out to be one of the most life altering days of my life. I'm forever grateful that they took the time to step into their role as Heaven's ambassadors and fulfill Jesus' commands to His disciples.

> *Matthew 10:7–8 (NAS): And as you go, preach, saying, 'The kingdom of heaven is at hand.' 8 "Heal the sick, raise the dead, cleanse the lepers, cast out demons. Freely you received, freely give.*

As introductions to the realm of the supernatural second heaven go, that was a doozy for a born-again worship leader from the Midwest who grew up in church. Let me also say that this is not a book on deliverance, nor am I glorifying Satan's activity or the power of demons in any way. I don't think we should go "hunt" them down and I don't think there's a demon hiding behind every garbage can or influencing every bad situation. But for me, this was a significant moment that revealed a dimension of reality that I'd only read about in Bible stories and seen fictionally portrayed in horror movies prior to this.

Suddenly, it all became real. It was scary, and I thought I was going crazy. This realm seemed out of control and overrun with powerful, spiteful beings intent on killing me, and that freaked me out. I, Matt Hugg, a church kid, a youth group leader, an undergraduate religion and philosophy student, born-again believer, and worship leader of one of the largest collegiate campus ministries in the country, had been walking through life with two unwanted house guests hiding in plain sight that were incessantly sabotaging me, my finances, my relationships, my work, my marriage, and I didn't even know they were there, much less how to get rid of them.

The experience prompted so many questions, "How could this gap have existed in my Christian experience and training??? Why couldn't I recognize them? How is it possible that I couldn't detect their presence? Why was I never taught about these creatures and how to get rid of them? Are there other people bound up like I was? Did I receive teaching about this but just miss it somewhere along the line?"

Practically, if the Devil and his demons were overtly "visible" to a believer, then they could be dealt with and their influence revoked much more easily. As a friend of mine likes to say, there is no junior Holy Spirit, and even a brand new follower of Jesus has been given authority to trample on these snakes. Their power comes from the fact that they operate in the shadows, cloaked in "normal" life, and therefore we have difficulty detecting their lies, binding them, and tearing down their works. Sadly, through systematic desensitization over generations, their influence has incrementally grown in our families and in the church. For decades, they've been slowly eroding the truth of scripture from our churches to where the Western Church considers the supernatural stories from the Bible to be exceptions instead of examples. This is an easy lie to believe because, on the surface, it seems true to our intellect. It has become too easy to read about Peter walking on water, Moses and a burning bush, Paul and the multitudes of healings and miraculous signs and wonders he performed, and to categorize them as completely "other" than ourselves.

We dare not remove the humanity of these Biblical heroes, nor disconnect our lives and experiences from theirs, or we risk losing the capacity, and the desire, to live the same sort of supernatural life they lived. They were flesh and bone, just like you and me. They ate, slept, got tired, got angry, told jokes, and did all the normal things you and I do. The era may be different, but greed, jealousy, sickness, famine, insecurity, jobs, money, taxes, etc. - they all remain basically unchanged to this day and throughout all human history. And let's not forget the most important fact, God himself, remains completely unchanged, unwavering, and eternal. Recalling what Jesus, the very Son of God, said in John 14:12.

> *John 14:12–14 (NLT): 12 "I tell you the truth, anyone who believes in me will do the same works I have done, and even greater works, because I am going to be with the Father. 13 You can ask for anything*

in my name, and I will do it, so that the Son can bring glory to the Father. 14 Yes, ask me for anything in my name, and I will do it!

With one, irrevocable, and unmistakably clear statement, Jesus makes it a part of the permanent, written record of Scripture, that ANYONE who believes in him will do the same works and even greater works than he did. In this passage, Jesus removes any excuse to disconnect my life, experiences, and reality from His. In this one sentence, I become totally responsible to heal lepers, open blind eyes and deaf ears, cast out demons, and raise the dead. I don't have the luxury of placing myself in some different category where I leave that stuff to preachers or prophets or other "professional" Christians.

I'm a king, following the King of Kings, and He just gave me an order. If I'm to be obedient, then I have to pursue this and not change the subject until I see the promised "same works and even greater works". Period.

Sadly, my kings, many of us have lost sight of this mandate from Heaven, and so we've reduced the wonder and adventure of Kingdom life to good behavior and boredom. We can read these passages over and over and breeze right past the weight of the responsibility that Jesus just placed on us. We almost subconsciously reject His invitation to intimate fellowship with the King of Kings and the incredible manifestation of authority, glory and power from the third-heaven that breaks into our first-heaven (Earth), and testifies of His glorious Kingdom.

While these demons seemed quite powerful based on their theatrics and hatefulness that day in the office, they were actually totally powerless against the name of Jesus spoken over me by my friends who had "eyes to see" and hearts to administer God's grace to me. I praise God that they did not take the easy path that day and simply let me go home, a slave to my unseen enemy.

Over the next several days, I felt a righteous anger begin to burn in me as I realized that the spirit of Religion that had infiltrated my world was to blame for my capture and imprisonment. I had been raised in a well-intentioned, but incomplete, religious environment that taught me only part of what I needed to know to win the battles of life. No good military training program would provide cadets with only partial combat training and then send them into battle. And yet, that is exactly what had happened. Let me be clear, I realize that our battle is not against flesh and blood and in no way is this a rant against the Church or anyone in it. With intense gratitude, I honor the spiritual mothers and fathers, and my biological mother and father, who imparted to me a value system and a foundation upon which my faith could grow. But I realized that day that Bitterness and Anger, among others, had been interfering in my life and had caused a lot of collateral, relational damage. Without an awareness of how to recognize and defeat them; it was no wonder I'd never been able to gain victory over so many giants in my life.

My blind spot was that I'd adopted an intellectual approach to faith that condemned experiential encounters with God as problematic because they are driven by feelings which cannot be trusted. As the saying goes, feelings make great servants but lousy masters, and while this is true, intellectualism is not without its own perilous pitfalls. It too is a terrible master. Inside an intellectual framework, demons can remain thoroughly concealed because the effects of their evil activities are easily attributed to other causes. I'd suggest that a spirit of intellectualism and religion has ransacked the church and its kings for generations right under our noses. If you don't believe me, consider this example. No modern Western doctor would sit with a patient and seriously consider that their fibromyalgia, autoimmune, diabetes, or cancer may be the result of a spiritual affliction, despite the fact that the hospital in which they practice medicine was likely started by a spirit-filled faith community and likely still bears a name like Lutheran, Methodist, St. Anthony, St. Luke, or St. Jude. Yet the doctors inside these hospitals largely ignore their patient's spiritual health in their practice and diagnosis.

Or imagine a chiropractor that diagnoses a patient's back pain as the result of having one leg shorter than the other. How many, do you suppose, would immediately pray that the shorter leg grows out as a treatment?

Instead, these medical professionals routinely prescribe drugs, perform physical adjustments, and their patients will probably be back. Any doctor who prayed as an initial approach to treatment, or even prayed to receive a spirit of revelation to get a strategic diagnosis and treatment, would likely be brought before a review board and fired.

Praying for healing seems ludicrous to our scientific mindset, sadly even for some in the church! Yet, I see legs grow out, deaf ears open, and people healed of diseases routinely at healing ministry services at our church. In my experience, churches like this are the exception, not the rule, and a whole generation of believers has been enslaved to a life without the manifest presence of the Holy Spirit and been convinced that it's normal. Kings are discovering that while this situation may be common, it is anything BUT "normal".

Before you categorize me as anti-medicine, please hear me out. I'm not advocating that we stop going to doctors and instead only pray for healing. On the contrary, I believe an inspired and Spirit filled medical community is one of the best representations of the Kingdom of Heaven on Earth. Doesn't it make sense that Holy Spirit would want to perform miracles AND create structures and systems that heal? Aren't advancements in our understanding of the human body and in medical treatments miracles in themselves? Why wouldn't He break in and perform miracles AND also commission His children to create Heaven-inspired structures and institutions that establish His Kingdom where they can work and fulfill their destiny?

I see bright spots of hope as I witness true kings step into their identity under the power of the Holy Spirit and into their assignments, whether as doctors, nurses, teachers, entrepreneurs, or preachers. And I'm grateful for that little Midwest city that was ground zero for my deliverance and for a powerful Word and Spirit led church there that is rapidly raising a new generation of Christ followers. They are Holy Spirit filled prophetic world-changers under wise and bold apostolic leadership. They've made it their mission and calling to send out servant hearted disciples with a passion for Jesus and the world. This church is not perfect, but that day I encountered the King and His Kingdom there as Heavenly ambassadors administered the true gospel of Jesus and I'm forever grateful.

ROUND 2... AND 3... AND 4... AND...

> *Matthew 12:43–45 (NAS): Now when the unclean spirit goes out of a man, it passes through waterless places seeking rest, and does not find it.*
>
> *44 "Then it says, 'I will return to my house from which I came'; and when it comes, it finds it unoccupied, swept, and put in order.*
>
> *45 "Then it goes and takes along with it seven other spirits more wicked than itself, and they go in and live there; and the last state of that man becomes worse than the first. That is the way it will also be with this evil generation."*

So yeah. I would love to tell you that from that day forward, I knew exactly how to spot and defeat my enemy and that I have been kicking his ass ever since. Not exactly.

It wasn't long before life served up another problem and guess who came back to join the pity party? You guessed it, Bitterness and Anger, those old familiar spirits were right there, ready to help me fall off the spiritual wagon. And I did. I became even more angry and embittered because of a failed business deal and a business associate who stole from me. Remember when I said Bitterness and Anger come in through the intellectual "gate"? This means that their suggestions appeal to our logical and rational minds. For example, it makes sense to seek retribution from people who cheat you in business, right? It makes sense to pay back evil for evil, right? This makes sense on paper, right?

I didn't know this at the time, but kings are masters at recognizing these lies as bait designed to trap believers in an earthbound "wisdom" that promises life, but actually leads to death. God's kings have become citizens of a different Kingdom and must internalize and obey Jesus' words in order to walk in the freedom, revelation and power of that Kingdom.

Matthew 5:38–48 (NAS): You have heard that it was said, 'An eye for an eye, and a tooth for a tooth.'

39 "But I say to you, do not resist an evil person; but whoever slaps you on your right cheek, turn the other to him also.

40 "If anyone wants to sue you and take your shirt, let him have your coat also.

41 "Whoever forces you to go one mile, go with him two.

42 "Give to him who asks of you, and do not turn away from him who wants to borrow from you.

43 "You have heard that it was said, 'You shall love your neighbor and hate your enemy.'

44 "But I say to you, love your enemies and pray for those who persecute you,

45 so that you may be sons of your Father who is in heaven; for He causes His sun to rise on the evil and the good, and sends rain on the righteous and the unrighteous.

46 "For if you love those who love you, what reward do you have? Do not even the tax collectors do the same?

47 "If you greet only your brothers, what more are you doing than others? Do not even the Gentiles do the same?

48 "Therefore you are to be perfect, as your heavenly Father is perfect

Before my deliverance experience, I thought this teaching was just about being a nicer person, but since then it has taken on new meaning. Could it be that these directions from Jesus are not about being nice, but are spiritual keys to remaining free from the influence of your mortal enemies like Bitterness, Anger, Victim, Religion, and others intent on killing you? I'd strongly suggest - YES!

Jesus isn't calling us into the gospel of "try harder, do better" or punishing us with another spiritual duty. He's giving us a powerful weapon to wield against the spiritual forces attempting to take us out.

However, for many of us, this passage is less about spiritual warfare and more about self-help or behavior modification. If that is our context, then we're doomed to stumble blindly through life, trying to be nicer in our own strength. We're bound to fail, and become discouraged and disillusioned. Your understanding of why Jesus issues these commands is critical to correct application of them on your own journey. In a battle where demons are bent on stealing, killing, and destroying us, these verses shift from good suggestions to non-negotiable tactics of warfare critical to defending ourselves.

My second deliverance experience was much like the first, except this time it took place at a weekend retreat, and a few of the same ministers were there to help me get free again.

The third experience was less intense, almost as if each time my enemies were losing their grasp as I learned to detect their lies before they took root in my mind.

The fourth experience I was able to be my own minister of freedom. Over time, I have learned to recognize their "voice", take their thoughts captive, and resist them. But make no mistake, they're never far and always waiting to jump into the conversation if I allow it. We understand the devil's tactics from Luke's record of Jesus' temptation in the desert.

Luke 4:13 (NAS): When the devil had finished every temptation, he left Him until an opportune time.

Like the devil, his demons wait for opportune moments when I'm weary, stressed, or have left my heart unguarded before they strike. Kings are good at detecting their presence and resisting their influence.

Kings, this is a good opportunity for some self-reflection to let the Spirit reveal if you are unknowingly being influenced by any unwanted house guests. If you feel you may be in some level of demonic bondage to Anger, Bitterness, Depression, Anxiety, Lust, Pride or others, I recommend you seek brothers in arms who can pray with you to receive freedom from these menaces. Allow Holy Spirit to inform this process for you, the timing, the people, and the place where you can walk this out. If you don't have a community that can help you walk through this, I recommend you seek a spiritual counselor who knows what to do and can help you get free. We also want to be a resource for you to receive healing, freedom, and power for this journey, and my team and I are available to pray with you. You can reach out to us for help at https://akingsfire.com My brothers and fellow kings, you are not alone.

Submit to the process and give yourself grace. Don't put this off. Get free. The longer you remain in bondage, the more destruction these demons will cause in your life. Your marriage, family relationships, and life could very well depend on it.

Last, as free men, as sons and kings, loyal to the King of Kings, embrace your responsibility to help others get free as you step into your destiny and partner with the plans and purposes of the Holy Spirit. Kings, your time has come to proclaim freedom to a world that is waiting for you. Let's roll.

Chapter 2

DEMON WOLVES

16"Look, I am sending you out as sheep among wolves. So be as shrewd as snakes and harmless as doves. 17 But beware! For you will be handed over to the courts and will be flogged with whips in the synagogues. 18 You will stand trial before governors and kings because you are my followers. But this will be your opportunity to tell the rulers and other unbelievers about me. 19When you are arrested, don't worry about how to respond or what to say. God will give you the right words at the right time. 20For it is not you who will be speaking—it will be the Spirit of your Father speaking through you.

—MATTHEW 10:15-20

I sat in the bathtub at about 4 am, up early again, unable to sleep. It had become my routine with the Lord. He'd wake me up and, as a prophetic symbolic action, He would request that I "soak" in His presence. So I'd get into the tub and soak out of obedience, sometimes for hours.

This morning He simply gave me one word - Operator. For the next several weeks I heard this word, and eventually I also heard a phrase, "1st, 2nd, 3rd, realm Operator".

During this time, my wife and I attended a conference where we live in Redding, CA and after one session, a man approached me I did not know. He told me that during worship, God had given him a word for me. The word was "Operator". Over the next several weeks, I came to understand that Holy Spirit was initiating me into a training program to teach me about the unseen realms in order to help me make sense of my past experiences and to help me navigate future assignments.

Let me begin by suggesting that we function in a world filled with wolves, as the passage above describes. Even as you read it, you may recall people you've encountered over the years, perhaps in a broken relationship, a failed business deal, the political arena, or even church. I'm not talking about those wolves and neither is Jesus.

Paul writes in Ephesians 6:12 that our battle is NOT against flesh and blood, but against evil rulers, authorities and powers in the UNSEEN world and evil spirits in Heaven-ly [literally: "Heaven-like"] places.

As a king, learning to recognize and navigate this unseen realm is entry-level kingship 101. It is a prerequisite to receiving your mantle of leadership and authority. I needed to go back to basic training with Holy Spirit because kings must be masters in the art of distinguishing the right enemy from the wrong one and the right battle from the wrong battle. People, for example, are never your enemy. Let me be clear about this, because I'm not sure you heard what I said. Politicians, or political parties with whom you disagree, are not your enemy. Your boss is not your enemy. Your spouse is not your enemy. You children are not your enemy. Neither your business competitor, nor the guy who stole from you, nor your neighbor, nor the cop who pulled you over last week, nor the Taliban terrorists that are presently plotting to kill you, nor any other human person on planet Earth is your enemy. If you don't internalize this truth, you'll never step fully into your role as Heaven's Ambassador. You'll not take seriously your responsibility to be the administrator of God's goodness and the gospel of reconciliation to ALL the Earth. Instead, you will reserve Heaven's goodness for people you love and proclaim the judgment of hell on people you hate. Kings can't pick and choose who God loves or who will be the next target of

His goodness and mercy. As C.S. Lewis said in his book, *The Weight of Glory,* "There are no ordinary people. You have never talked to a mere mortal." Indeed, Saul, the first century persecutor of Christ's followers - a literal terrorist - became one of the most powerful, Holy Spirit-filled warrior kings to walk the earth, and author of roughly one half of the New Testament. We never know who God is targeting for His radical love and blessings and we dare not disqualify any human as we steward the grace and abundance of Heaven.

Humans are image bearers of the Almighty God, fearfully and wonderfully made, created intentionally by their loving Heavenly Father - yes, even "woke" cancel culture activists, politicians, terrorists and your cranky co-workers who may not know Jesus yet. Kings know and respect that reality. Yes, we are born as slaves to sin and in bondage to greed, lust, addictions, and lost in pride. But this simply spotlights the necessity for kings to hone their spiritual senses to discern ALL the players in every circumstance - both the seen and unseen parties. If we can do this well, then we will "see" the person through Heaven's eyes, be empowered to love them instead of judge them, and maybe even play a role in their spiritual journey toward freedom.

WE NEVER KNOW WHO GOD IS TARGETING FOR HIS RADICAL LOVE AND BLESSINGS AND WE DARE NOT DISQUALIFY ANY HUMAN AS WE STEWARD THE GRACE AND ABUNDANCE OF HEAVEN.

As a young man, my inability to navigate this realm and gain victory caused me to misjudge people constantly. It also caused me to fall into sin, temptation, and addiction repeatedly. My early life as a believer included a tremendous amount of pain and shame over sin and addictions I couldn't overcome, along with the creation of a brilliantly crafted persona for people to see and enjoy from the outside. It was so normal that I was honestly unaware of just how much energy I devoted to posturing, pretending, and hiding who I really was. And my own self-judgment for my failures in my inner world made me a judgmental critic of all people who couldn't "perform" as I thought they should. Sound familiar?

You and I have real enemies that are disembodied spirits - demons - and they don't like us. They occupy time and space in an unseen realm that is overlaid and intertwined with this Earthly realm and can move through regions, cities, homes, and rooms. They can possess people, as we see with the Garasene Demoniac in Mark 5, and can oppress believers as my own personal experience confirms.

Whatever form of influence they may have, as a believer, you have authority AND power over them. Authority and power are different things. As one of my spiritual mentors likes to say, authority is the police badge, the power is the gun.

This all makes sense in theory and as a child I can even recall singing songs like "There is power, power, wonder-working power, in the blood of the Lamb!". While the words of these songs are true, they do little to teach the practical, real-world tactics kings must master in order to achieve victory over these foes. You can sing the national anthem with everything you've got, but in a war, you need training to understand how to use your weapon, fight your enemy, and win.

We're about to go deep into scripture to unpack this important reality. Follow this track with me, because it's essential to understand the practical changes that took place inside you when you became a born again Christ-follower and how you are now a participant in this unseen realm with a very important role to play.

This may seem elementary for some of you, but indulge me while I outline the basic gospel to provide context. As my experience confirms; just because we prayed "the prayer" in church, got baptized, or went to youth group as a kid doesn't mean there aren't potentially gaping holes in our understanding of our new life in Christ. Fortunately, the Holy Spirit, the master teacher, is kind and patient with us in the learning process.

When you became a follower of Christ through his atoning work on the cross, you received forgiveness and became an adopted son in his family.

> *Ephesians 1:5 (NLT): 5 God decided in advance to adopt us into his own family by bringing us to himself through Jesus Christ. This is what he wanted to do, and it gave him great pleasure.*

Except this is not just any family, it's THE Royal Family for all time. As the newborn son of the King you are automatically a prince - a king in training. In a miraculous spiritual birthing process, your sin was forgiven, your identity was upgraded from a subject of the kingdom of darkness where you were a slave to sin, to cherished son in the family and in the Kingdom of Heaven. You literally became a co-heir (brother) with Jesus. Paul explains this beautifully in Romans. Read it. It's essential to know who you have become in and through Christ. Without this understanding, you might as well join a country club instead of a church.

> *2 Corinthians 5:17 (NLT): 17 This means that anyone who belongs to Christ has become a new person. The old life is gone; a new life has begun!*

If you don't fully realize that you're a new creation (1 Cor 5:17) with a job to do, then I'm afraid your "Christian" experience will probably devolve into boredom. Your energy will be spent shopping around for a place where you can get comfortable with the music, preacher, and the people instead of passionately pursuing your royal assignment to be an enforcer of God's will on Earth.

The analogy of birth can get weird for men, as we see with Nicodemus' dialogue with Jesus in John 3:3. But it's the exact right analogy, because it's not an analogy at all - it's precisely what happens. Your spiritual birth is important because it establishes your royal birthright. That is why Jesus mandates being born again as a prerequisite for entrance into the Kingdom. Birth is not a metaphor. It is the reality of what took place for you to begin spiritual life in the second and third heaven in the same way that your physical birth is a necessary first step for you to begin life on Earth. When you were born into the Earth, you became the de facto heir to everything your parents own. It is the same with your spiritual birth in the second and third realm. These additional two dimensions are not fiction or myth. They are real and as a spiritual son of the King of Kings it is your pleasure and joy to not only become aware of them, but to navigate them, and partner with the Holy Spirit to discover your royal inheritance and build God's kingdom so that the realities of Heaven become the realities of Earth. You were born to be a 1st, 2nd, and 3rd realm Operator.

At the moment of your spiritual birth, you inherit this royal identity simply because of who your father is. That's how monarchies work. I know this is simplistic, but as Westerners, we have little practical experience with this kind of government and therefore its effects on our identity and impact on our daily lives can get lost in theory, so I'll spend a bit of time unpacking this.

Why is birthright in a Kingdom important?

When Jesus walked the Earth, he shared unbroken fellowship with his Father via the Spirit of God, which came upon him after his baptism, and his royal identity was confirmed by God's own words.

> *Matthew 3:16–17 (NLT): After his baptism, as Jesus came up out of the water, the heavens were opened and he saw the Spirit of God descending like a dove and settling on him. 17 And a voice from heaven said, "This is my dearly loved Son, who brings me great joy."*

Did you catch all that? After baptism *(baptism is the prophetic action of being spiritually born)* the Holy Spirit came upon Him *(Holy Spirit is His Heavenly birth certificate that established His citizenship in the Kingdom of Heaven)* and His father declared, "This is my dearly loved Son, who brings me great joy", which was the affirmation of His identity as a member of God's family.

This scene shouldn't seem unfamiliar. For those of you who have experienced the birth of your own children, perhaps you can recall the scene when your own son or daughter was born. They emerged from the womb into the world on a specific day that you've celebrated ever since as their birthday. You signed papers that became official documents, their birth certificate establishing them as citizens with all the rights and privileges that come with that. And you probably recall a tender moment where you looked at your beloved child and whispered some phrase, some declaration of your love over them like, "You're mine, I love you, I will always love you and protect you."

Does the baptism of Jesus take on new significance as you view it through this lense? It should, and so should, your own spiritual birth. Perhaps there were no booming voices from heaven on the day you were born again, but make no mistake, the Father spoke the same words over you on that day. Heaven rejoiced to receive another son into the family, and Holy Spirit was given to you to confirm your citizenship in the exact same way.

I'd suggest that Jesus functioned masterfully out of this Heavenly identity and therefore had access to the superior power available in this 3rd Heaven realm. His "supernatural" ability to defy laws of nature, perform miracles, signs and wonders, and speak incredible revelatory wisdom came from His intimate connection with His Father and His position in His Father's Heavenly Kingdom where this kind of activity was "natural". Moreover, when Jesus completed His earthly mission and won victory over Satan - even over death - God elevated Him and gave Him all authority in heaven, on the earth, and under the earth. Jesus explains this reality in His parting words and commissioning of His disciples.

> *Matthew 28:18–20 (NLT): Jesus came and told his disciples, "I have been given all authority in heaven and on earth. 19 Therefore, go and make disciples of all the nations, baptizing them in the name of the Father and the Son and the Holy Spirit. 20 Teach these new disciples to obey all the commands I have given you. And be sure of this: I am with you always, even to the end of the age."*

Since you have put your faith in Jesus and have been born again, God the Father has granted you that SAME intimate connection with Him, and citizenship in Heaven via the SAME Spirit Jesus had.

> *Ephesians 1:13–14 (NLT): And now you Gentiles have also heard the truth, the Good News that God saves you. <u>And when you believed in Christ, he identified you as his own by giving you the Holy Spirit, whom he promised long ago. 14 The Spirit is God's guarantee that he will give us the inheritance he promised and that he has purchased us to be his own people.</u> He did this so we would praise and glorify him.*

In addition, we are granted a share of Jesus' inheritance, his birthright of power, and authority. You have a position in God's family, and therefore also have an identity and authority in His Kingdom.

> *Ephesians 2:6 (NLT): For he raised us from the dead along with Christ and seated us with him in the heavenly realms because we are united with Christ Jesus.*

Still tracking? I hope so because this is astonishing! The proof of this birthright is the Holy Spirit, who has cleansed us from all sin, come to live inside us, and fused himself together with our spirit, making us eternal citizens of God's Kingdom.

Holy Spirit's presence in the life of a believer IS DETECTABLE by signs, wonders, miracles, and the fruits of love, joy, peace, patience, kindness, goodness, faithfulness, gentleness, self-control, unity, tongues, revelation, boldness, and many others identified throughout scripture. Paul declares in 1 Corinthians 6:19 that our physical bodies are the "temple" of the Holy Spirit. This is the same Spirit that created the heavens and the earth, and the same Spirit that descended on Jesus after his baptism, the same Spirit that opened blind eyes, healed the sick, proclaimed the Kingdom, raised Jesus from the dead, and fell at Pentecost.

This is the same Spirit that destroys the works of the devil and his demons, makes us fearless, and, most importantly, this is the Spirit of adoption by which we can cry out to our Heavenly Father.

> *Romans 8:15–17 (NLT): So you have not received a spirit that makes you fearful slaves. Instead, you received God's Spirit when he adopted you as his own children. Now we call him, "Abba, Father." 16 For his Spirit joins with our spirit to affirm that we are God's children. 17 And since we are his children, we are his heirs. In fact, together with Christ we are heirs of God's glory. But if we are to share his glory, we must also share his suffering.*

I know that was a deluge of scripture. I hope you connected all the spiritual dots and have started to realize the significance of what took place when you said "Yes" to Jesus and were born again. You did a lot more than simply join a church! Your citizenship was transferred into a new eternal realm and you were adopted into the family of the all powerful, all knowing, all loving King of Kings - ruler of the Heavens and the Earth - for all eternity.

Now then, from this new identity and position, we get to partner with the Holy Spirit in our day-to-day Earthly life to carry out the amazing assignments our King has for us. What???? How???? Don't worry. We're going to attempt to demystify this process. You don't have to be a philosopher or theologian to figure it out. Holy Spirit has made this quite simple and intensely practical.

Holy Spirit trains us how to think better thoughts by renewing our mind to align with the superior reality of Heaven. From there, He teaches us how to use our new identity and the authority that comes with it to shift our environment to look more like heaven. In this process, He empowers us to detect and revoke the influence of Satan and his demons. This training and teaching process begins the day you make Jesus Lord of your life and continues throughout your life on Earth. As my dad likes to say, "If you're not dead, you're not done."

Holy Spirit uses all means necessary to teach us, including scripture, worship, teaching, mentors, our physical world, spiritual encounters, dreams, visions, and through the circumstances of our lives - good, bad and ugly. And don't worry, He is committed to this process even more than we are and He is a scandalously kind and patient teacher.

This training is important because being spiritually born again into this amazing family with this amazing power is like being given a Lamborghini. But just because you have the keys doesn't mean you know how to drive it, much less win races. A good father knows you need training before you try to hit top speed so you don't hurt yourself and others around you. Up to this point, you've heard me allude to different 1st, 2nd, and 3rd realms of existence. In the next section, we'll explore the three realms and how we function in each.

THE REALMS

First let me say that my understanding of the three realms, or "Heavens" as the Scriptures call them, is just that - my understanding. While I believe it is true, and supported by Scripture, I realize there are other theories about our unseen spiritual reality held by really smart people who've probably done a lot more research than me. Therefore, I humbly present the following as my current best understanding of how the Earthly physical realm, the unseen spiritual realm, and the Kingdom of Heaven are intertwined and how we engage with each.

The Bible describes these as "Heavens" (plural) and they are referenced in many places, including the Genesis account of creation. As a born-again believer in Jesus, the Spirit of God has uniquely positioned you into these realms, whether you realize it or not. They are:

- Earth Realm, also sometimes referred to as the "First Heaven". This realm is referenced contextually throughout scripture and comprises the Earth, atmosphere, sun, moon, stars, and other physical, observable elements. It's the realm that is fixed in time and space and governed by physical natural laws like gravity. Obviously, this is the realm you were physically born into on your birthday and you interact with it using your five physical senses. It can be vividly observed, experienced, and understood through your intellectual brain, mind, will, and emotions, and to a lesser degree, your imagination and intuition.
- Unseen Realm - referred to as the "Second Heaven" in the Bible. This is the realm you can perceive with your spirit, your mind's eye, and your imagination. Sometimes people refer to these collectively as your "sixth sense". As you tune your physical senses, you can also begin to perceive this realm through your physical senses like smell, sight, hearing and touch. This is the theatre of war where the kingdom of darkness and God's Kingdom clash. This realm is occupied by many unseen actors, including angels and demons. However, as referenced above, they can manifest physically, be seen visually, and be heard audibly, as anyone who's interacted with an angel or demon can attest. We are presently involved in a "struggle" against evil actors in this realm, as Paul teaches in Ephesians 6:12.

  Ephesians 6:12 (NAS): For our struggle is not against flesh and blood, but against the rulers, against the powers, against the world forces of this darkness, against the spiritual forces of wickedness in the heavenly places.

In this realm Satan has authority as described in 2 Cor. 4:4 and Eph. 2:2.

> *2 Corinthians 4:3–4 (NLT): 3 If the Good News we preach is hidden behind a veil, it is hidden only from people who are perishing. 4 Satan, who is the god of this world, has blinded the minds of those who don't believe. They are unable to see the glorious light of the Good News. They don't understand this message about the glory of Christ, who is the exact likeness of God.*

> *Ephesians 2:2 (NLT): 2 You used to live in sin, just like the rest of the world, obeying the devil—the commander of the powers in the unseen world. He is the spirit at work in the hearts of those who refuse to obey God.*

He was granted this authority by Adam and Eve in Genesis 3 through deception whereby they were tricked into disobeying a direct command from God, and instead they obeyed Satan. In so doing, they defected from God's Kingdom and unwittingly becoming trapped in Satan's kingdom.

- Highest Heaven - called the "third heaven". Paul recalls his spiritual experiences of this realm in 2 Cor. 12:2 and describes our position there alongside Jesus in Eph 2:6.

> *2 Corinthians 12:2–4 (NLT): 2 I was caught up to the third heaven fourteen years ago. Whether I was in my body or out of my body, I don't know—only God knows. 3 Yes, only God knows whether I was in my body or outside my body. But I do know 4 that I was caught up to paradise and heard things so astounding that they cannot be expressed in words, things no human is allowed to tell.*

Ephesians 2:6 (NLT): 6 For he raised us from the dead along with Christ and seated us with him in the heavenly realms because we are united with Christ Jesus.

This is the realm where God's supreme reign is ALWAYS manifested, so there is no sickness, poverty, lack, or evil influence of any kind. We're seated here for a reason. Like Paul, our spirits can ascend spiritually to this realm to meet with the Father and Jesus in fellowship. This is the realm Jesus connected deeply to during his Earthly life when he would go away to pray to his Father as he often did. Jesus' true spiritual identity, nature, and heavenly glory in this realm were seen visibly by a few disciples at the transfiguration event recorded in Matthew's Gospel. In addition, we see Jesus was not alone in this realm, but could fellowship with saints who had gone before him, including Moses and Elijah.

Matthew 17:1–9 (AMP): AND SIX days after this, Jesus took with Him Peter and James and John his brother, and led them up on a high mountain by themselves.

2 And His appearance underwent a change in their presence; and His face shone clear and bright like the sun, and His clothing became as white as light.

3 And behold, there appeared to them Moses and Elijah, who kept talking with Him.

4 Then Peter began to speak and said to Jesus, Lord, it is good and delightful that we are here; if You approve, I will put up three booths here—one for You and one for Moses and one for Elijah.

5 While he was still speaking, behold, a shining cloud [composed of light] overshadowed them, and a voice from the cloud said, This is My Son, My Beloved, with Whom

> *I am [and have always been] delighted. Listen to Him! [Ps. 2:7; Isa. 42:1.]*
>
> *6 When the disciples heard it, they fell on their faces and were seized with alarm and struck with fear.*
>
> *7 But Jesus came and touched them and said, Get up, and do not be afraid.*
>
> *8 And when they raised their eyes, they saw no one but Jesus only.*
>
> *9 And as they were going down the mountain, Jesus cautioned and commanded them, Do not mention to anyone what you have seen, until the Son of Man has been raised from the dead*

> This realm is radiating with terrifying power and glory and is our single source of all spiritual blessings, power, wisdom, and revelation, just as it was for our big brother Jesus when He walked the Earth as a man. When Jesus taught his disciples how to pray in Matthew 6:10, he instructed us to pray "on earth, as it is in Heaven" because he wanted to have us bring the realities of this third Heaven realm into the Earth - just like He did.

It's also important to note that Satan, formerly Lucifer, was one of three archangels that ministered to God prior to creation and was thrown out of this realm as Jesus references in John 10:18 when he describes the scene where he saw "Satan fall from Heaven like lightning". In Revelation 12:4, we also see that ⅓ of the angels, presumably those under his command, also were cast down to Earth. So how many demons are there? Difficult to say. Some translations of Hebrews 12:22 tell us that angels are "countless multitudes", so it's a bit unclear just how many demons are running around the Earth. Let's assume there are a lot, and they're under the command of a fallen archangel who hates humankind.

Jesus declares in John 12:31 that the judgment has come upon the world and the "ruler of this world will be cast out" and throughout His ministry He establishes authority over the second realm and the unseen demonic beings that cause illness, pain, blindness, and wreak havoc on humankind. On occasions, He even can force unseen demons to manifest their form in the first realm by making them speak, or silencing their speech, sending them into pigs, and in various other ways. I believe Jesus did this to pull back the veil to the second realm so that His disciples could learn the nature and tactics of these beings. Call it tactical battle training for their future exploits with Him, and also for their future after Pentecost.

Jesus goes to great lengths to describe the realities of this realm, to reveal it for what it is, and to teach His disciples the tactics required to engage, fight, and win. And in an absolutely incredible command in Matthew 10:8, He commands us to heal the sick, raise the dead, cleanse the lepers, cast out demons. Even more incredibly, He tells His own disciples in John 14:12 that anyone who believes in Him will do the same works, and *even greater works*, than He did! He has more confidence in us than we have in ourselves for sure! But as we walk in step with Holy Spirit living inside us, we're learning to step into our destiny as world-changers with the power and wisdom of Heaven - fighting ONLY the battles, and ONLY the beings He commissions us to. This authority doesn't give us permission to be loose cannons binding and loosing every demon or demonic stronghold we encounter. As kings under the direct command of the King of Kings, we recognize that our life is not our own and we're not fighting for our own glory. We're on assignment. We fight when Holy Spirit says fight, and we stand down when He tells us to stand down.

The Bible actually has a LOT to teach us about these realms. Every supernatural event recorded in the Scripture shows the interaction between these realms and there are hundreds of them. Jesus leaves no doubts about His expectations of how His followers are to function in all three realms. He talked about them and engaged with all three realms constantly. Paul and the apostles further expand our awareness and understanding of these realms as the Church age was born after Pentecost. These events captured in the Scriptures, combined with testimonies of believers throughout history, and our own firsthand experiences, create the framework for us to understand the role we play as kings positioned inter-dimensionally in all three realms.

AMID THESE DARK DAYS, I'M FILLED WITH A SUPERNATURAL HOPE THAT DEFIES ALL EARTHBOUND RATIONAL AND LOGIC. A FIRE BURNS IN MY GUT TO UNLEASH HEAVEN ON THE EARTH

As we've learned, Earth is currently governed by Satan and his demonic strongholds and principalities in the second heaven stand in the way of God's Kingdom fully manifesting on Earth. Don't misunderstand this dynamic, God has all authority and power - He has asserted, and will continue to assert His supreme authority at any moment He chooses. But Jesus clarified that the Father's intent is to co-labor with His sons - kings - to manifest the realities of Heaven on the Earth through the same signs, miracles, and wonders that He performed. His parting words to His followers in Mark are a stunning commission to engage and advance.

> *Mark 16:15–18 (NAS): And He said to them, "Go into all the world and preach the gospel to all creation.*
>
> *16 "He who has believed and has been baptized shall be saved; but he who has disbelieved shall be condemned.*
>
> *17 "These signs will accompany those who have believed: in My name they will cast out demons, they will speak with new tongues;*
>
> *18 They will pick up serpents, and if they drink any deadly poison, it will not hurt them; they will lay hands on the sick, and they will recover."*

When Jesus' brothers (that's us) don't own this responsibility, then the Earth and humankind suffer under the evil and tyrannical rule of Satan and his savage demons. It doesn't take a genius to observe this reality. Just turn on the news. It's a 24-hour cycle of evil on parade, visible in the pain of wars, the horror of murders, abuse, and corruption that all find their source in a fallen archangel, hell-bent on destroying humankind.

Kings, this is what you were born for. I believe we're at a profound moment in history and amid these dark days, I'm filled with a supernatural hope that defies all earthbound rationale and logic. A fire burns in my gut to unleash Heaven on the Earth and to fill the Heavens with the sound of His praises, the testimonies of His goodness, and the glory of His Kingdom. As kings in His Kingdom, we have a mandate and profound purpose to liberate Earth, set captives free, and proclaim the Kingdom is near. Our power flows from our inherited royal identity, our placement in Heaven WITH Christ, and the intimate friendship we share with Holy Spirit. Jesus' mandate, which He identified in Isaiah 61, is still our mandate today.

> *Luke 4:14–19 (AMP): Then Jesus went back full of and under the power of the [Holy] Spirit into Galilee, and the fame of Him spread through the whole region round about.*
>
> *15 And He Himself conducted [a course of] teaching in their synagogues, being recognized and honored and praised by all.*
>
> *16 So He came to Nazareth, [that Nazareth] where He had been brought up, and He entered the synagogue, as was His custom on the Sabbath day. And He stood up to read.*
>
> *17 And there was handed to Him [the roll of] the book of the prophet Isaiah. He opened (unrolled) the book and found the place where it was written, [Isa. 61:1, 2.]*
>
> *18 The Spirit of the Lord [is] upon Me, because He has anointed Me [the Anointed One, the Messiah] to preach the good news (the Gospel) to the poor; He has sent Me to announce release to*

> *the captives and recovery of sight to the blind, to send forth as delivered those who are oppressed [who are downtrodden, bruised, crushed, and broken down by calamity],*
>
> *19 To proclaim the accepted and acceptable year of the Lord [the day when salvation and the free favors of God profusely abound.] [Isa. 61:1, 2.]*

I hope you're as excited as I am about accepting this mandate, putting on your mantle of authority, and discovering the power, tactics, and resources available to us. We are divinely positioned to set captives free in the same ways, and even greater ways, than Jesus did. As my friend and mentor Steve shared many times during our decade of ministry together, our job is to find and rescue our family members currently trapped by our enemy. Kings, our divine destiny awaits. Are you in?

WHAT ABOUT WEAPONS?

History books are full of stories of Earthly monarchies that were stolen because young kings were ill-equipped to defend their territory and crown. While they inherited their father's kingdom through birthright, they couldn't hold on to it because they couldn't effectively wield the weapons necessary to defend it. We need to take spiritual lessons from these Earthly examples. The good news for us is that the Holy Spirit is committed to training us in warfare to not only maintain stability and peace, but to advance and expand His Kingdom.

WEAPONS QUICK LIST:

- Worship. Worship IS actually a weapon, and demons can't stand the sound of it. Imagine fingernails on a chalkboard! I believe worship actually has a metaphysical negative effect on them. It pierces and rings in their ears to such a painful degree that eventually they have to leave when it is sung into the atmosphere.

- Intimacy - one-on-one time spent listening and praying
- Rest - literal sleep, but also stillness and downtime
- Jesus' Name. The Bible goes out of its way to describe the supremacy of the name of Jesus, and how it is the name ABOVE all other names. To make this abundantly clear, Paul tells the Philippians the following.

  Philippians 2:9–11 (NLT): Therefore, God elevated him to the place of highest honor and gave him the name above all other names, 10 that at the name of Jesus every knee should bow, in heaven and on earth and under the earth, 11 and every tongue declare that Jesus Christ is Lord, to the glory of God the Father.

- Scripture. Jesus' wilderness temptation was His first recorded "test" after His baptism by John, His Father's commissioning, and the Holy Spirit came upon Him. And good news, He passed His test with flying colors by quoting scripture. In the Gospels of Matthew, Mark, and Luke, the Devil attempts to sabotage Jesus by lying to Him, twisting scripture, and manipulation - in much the same way he sabotaged Adam and Eve. But unlike Adam and Eve, Jesus was able - through partnership with the Holy Spirit's help - to recall scriptures that exposed the deception and unraveled the Devil's attacks with the truth of God's word.
- Fruits of Spirit. Galatians 5:22 tells us:

  Galatians 5:22–23 (AMP): But the fruit of the [Holy] Spirit [the work which His presence within accomplishes]

> *is love, joy (gladness), peace, patience (an even temper, forbearance), kindness, goodness (benevolence), faithfulness,*
>
> *23 Gentleness (meekness, humility), self-control (self-restraint, continence). Against such things there is no law [that can bring a charge].*

Reality is that there is no spiritual force that works against the fruit of the spirit. The last sentence in verse 23 says, "Against such things, there is no law [that can bring a charge]." Simply put, if you manifest these fruits in your life and relationships, there is nothing that can ever be said, claimed, or charged against you. It's like spiritual teflon for the devil and his demons. They can try to attack you, but when you flow with fruit of the spirit, nothing "sticks."

- Gifts of the Spirit. (1 Cor. 12)
- Authentic community as the "Body of Christ" (1 Cor. 12:27)
- Many, many others...

In future chapters, we'll unpack these and others in greater detail. But undoubtedly the best weapon of all is the indwelling power and presence of the Holy Spirit Himself. He is the very Spirit of God, that raised Christ from the dead, that was there at the beginning and spoke galaxies into existence, and He is our ever-present companion for the rest of eternity. Even in the Matthew passage we used to open Chapter 1, Jesus says that the Spirit of God will provide words to speak when we stand before kings and rulers and, moreover, that it will be God speaking. The Word of God is the uncontested supreme authority in every situation and carries with it the power to accomplish whatever He states. It's a weapon that simply can not be defeated.

It's important we learn the correct weapons because if we fight giants with a sword, then we fight on their terms and with weapons they are familiar with. However, if we fight a giant with a small, accurately placed stone traveling at incredible speed, then we can inflict a mortal wound that they never see coming.

Kings understand that the weapons of our warfare are not carnal, worldly weapons. On the night Judas betrayed Jesus, Peter attempted to take matters into his own hands and wielded a weapon common to his enemies when he inflicted a minor wound on the high priest's servant. Jesus admonished Peter to put his sword away, healed the ear of the priest, and then launched an incredible and unorthodox counter-attack on Satan. Through His surrender to the cross, Jesus completely ANNIHILATED death itself along with every other work of the Devil for all humankind for all time. I bet the Devil didn't see that one coming.

So next time you're tempted to get angry because someone has become angry at you, don't. Instead, ask Holy Spirit which weapon you need to diffuse and defeat the enemy's attack. Kings have weapons at our disposal that the enemy can't beat, including: prayer, worship, kindness, supernatural miraculous power, among many others. Picking up the weapon of forgiveness and worship when you're viciously attacked with anger and betrayal confounds the enemy as he loses control over the situation and is forced to disengage. Kings who become masters in this form of warfare represent the greatest danger to the kingdom of darkness, because they have the greatest authority in the Kingdom of Heaven.

In 1st Samuel, we learn that Jonathan and Saul are the only ones among the Israelite people who have swords because there are no blacksmiths in the land. So Israelites had to purchase weapons from their enemies - the Philistines - in order to fight the Philistines! This was an ill-advised strategy, inherently flawed. You don't fight your enemy with HIS weapons, which he will always wield better than you. You gain authority by training with the weapons of your Kingdom in accordance with the tactics and strategies of Heaven, if you want to win. On the surface, this is often counterintuitive, but trust me - it's ALWAYS the right decision. You've heard the saying don't bring a knife to a gunfight, but I'd argue that as a king, that's exactly what you do. When He tells you to march around Jericho seven times and shout in order to conquer it, you do it, regardless of how ridiculous it may seem, and you watch him deliver the city into your hands. When He tells you to worship in the middle of the night in your prison cell, you do it, and then you watch His earthquake bring down the house. And when Holy Spirit tells you to bring a sling and a stone to a sword fight, you do it and watch the giant fall before you.

YOU GAIN AUTHORITY BY TRAINING WITH THE WEAPONS OF YOUR KINGDOM IN ACCORDANCE WITH THE TACTICS AND STRATEGIES OF HEAVEN, IF YOU WANT TO WIN.

By now, you might be trying to wrap your head around a couple of conflicting ideas and questions. If we have all these weapons, advantages, help from Holy Spirit, and inherited royal authority, why do we still face battles and lose?

Let's explore that question for a moment.

- Authority = Badge.
- Worship, Jesus' name, Holy Spirit's power, and the others listed above = weapons.
- You and I = passive, unaware, blind, untrained, deceived, fearful, faithless, disconnected.

Ouch!! Sorry, not sorry. Kings, we need to acknowledge the truth about ourselves. I know it's true for many of you because it was, and often still is, true of me.

Imagine a police officer who happens to be at a convenience store right as the store is being robbed. He has the authority to do something, and he has all the weapons to subdue the perpetrator. But he has a choice whether to engage. If he doesn't see the crime taking place, or if he sees it but decides that it's just a normal part of life, or if he becomes scared because of lack of training, then the perp takes what he wants, gets away, and the store owner becomes a victim.

Sadly, the above scenario describes a spiritual reality for many of us. Most of us fall into some/all of these categories.

- Unaware
- Untrained
- Unconcerned
- Fearful

The fact is that Jesus knew very well what He was talking about in the Matthew 10:15 passage. He wants His Kings to KNOW that they're functioning in an environment where there are "wolves" and they have power to sabotage us. Moreover, He wants His kings to take ownership of their training.

If we pour the Word of God into our minds and hearts, and align our thoughts and heart with our royal identity, and if we pray for spiritual sensitivity to discern the movements of Holy Spirit and the tactics of our unseen enemies, then we can begin to frustrate their plans, tear down their works and fortify our homes, families, businesses, health, and every area of our lives. Jesus died to give you life and victory in THIS life AND the afterlife. Your salvation is not just a future-state reality. Your spiritual birth launched you into eternal Kingdom life and citizenship immediately. Sadly, many of us have spent years trapped in a hopeless, defeated life and not living in freedom and power that is our inheritance. But no longer.

I see us growing together and I'm elated to see so many of my brothers embracing this mission and calling in ways our world has never seen. I'm excited to band together with fellow kings committed to discovering their anointing and purpose. I'm eager to sit with the Master teacher, the Holy Spirit, while He trains me to navigate the unseen realm and how to wield His weapons.

To really dive into this as a part of your personal journey, I recommend studying Paul's letters, and then doubling back to the Gospels to see how the apostles and Jesus navigated our 1st, 2nd, and 3rd heaven reality. Re-reading these Scriptures through your new lenses of royal identity and supernatural citizenship will be amazing - like reading them for the first time - as new details in each story leap off the pages and Holy Spirit reveals who He is, and who you are in His-story.

In these texts, we see so many strategies and weapons Holy Spirit directs Jesus and the Apostles to use for different battles and we will do likewise. One day, we may read the scriptures to build courage or gain a specific strategy for a specific situation. Maybe the next day we'll need to recall a prophetic word we received or Holy Spirit will give us visions, images, or words, as we meditate. Another day, the battle may require us to jump around our house singing and shouting in worship. Often I'll pray in tongues just to bypass my intellectual mind and go straight into a place of connection with Holy Spirit. Sometimes all the above!

Whatever the battle du jour requires, Holy Spirit will be our Master teacher as we dedicate time to this process. As we cultivate the ability to hear and sense His directives, we'll understand how to navigate the unseen realm and operate as Jesus commands... as shrewd as a snake, but as innocent as a dove.

I pray for us to have new spiritual "eyes" as we read His scripture and gain practical wisdom and revelatory strategies to advance His Kingdom in this war zone called Earth.

Chapter 3

WORK. DO IT.

Dear friends, you always followed my instructions when I was with you. And now that I am away, it is even more important. Work hard to show the results of your salvation, obeying God with deep reverence and fear. 13 For God is working in you, giving you the desire and the power to do what pleases him. 14 Do everything without complaining and arguing, 15 so that no one can criticize you. Live clean, innocent lives as children of God, shining like bright lights in a world full of crooked and perverse people.

—PHILIPPIANS 2:12–15 (NLT)

Work hard. There it is, in black and white. Kings, you're welcome. You have permission to be driven, to work, to pour out your lives, to sweat, plow, and push. Move forcefully and joyfully. Be a contributor as you move, shake, and hustle. And the nobility of this work is that it proves your salvation. There you go. All you high-capacity kings who need a dragon to slay, a mountain to conquer, people to lead; Paul has given you permission to run like the thoroughbreds that you are. Use your skills, competency, your natural abilities and charisma to impact the environment around you and forcefully advance.

There are only a few conditions to this exhortation to work hard... and they're doozies.

The primary condition is that you work hard *while* obeying God with deep reverence and fear. So before all you aspiring workaholics (like me) throw yourself headlong into your work, I'd like to unpack this profound exhortation. The guard rails around your work are always reverence and obedience to God and what keeps those guard rails in razor-sharp focus is a deep intimacy with Holy Spirit. This is a critical condition for all God's children, but especially for high-achievers, not because we're so much better than others - quite the opposite. A highly anointed, gifted, overachiever without self-control can do a lot of damage in a hurry to themselves and those around them, which is why surrendering our skills, abilities, and work to a higher authority is necessary. Kings are powerful in the same way a gun is powerful. Under the right authority, they're a profound blessing to all around them and provide safety and lasting peace. Under the wrong authority, they're dangerous and devastating.

THE GUARD RAILS AROUND YOUR WORK ARE ALWAYS REVERENCE AND OBEDIENCE TO GOD AND WHAT KEEPS THOSE GUARD RAILS IN RAZOR-SHARP FOCUS IS A DEEP INTIMACY WITH HOLY SPIRIT.

I'm an entrepreneur. I'm self-motivated, eager, hard-working, and capable. And in the past, I've loved to pretend that everything I was doing was work "unto the Lord" even when it wasn't. Most of the time, I was honestly unaware that my motives were flawed, self-seeking, and rooted in insecurity. In the past, I would read right past the most important part of this passage - obedience, based on deep reverence, and even fear. I'd crash through the guard rails around this command to work hard and put on the "try harder, do better" gospel and get after it!

As a go-getter, I've never been too afraid of failure. I'm drawn to the challenge and the impossible situations. So when I'm commanded to work in a state of reverence and fear, I honestly disconnect a bit. This disconnection from fear and reverence for God's will in my work has had consequences. I have had to endure many seasons of failure and frustration where my work seemed fruitless and caused people around me intense loss and pain. Why?

I believe God, in His mercy, allows seasons like this to teach us how His kingdom works. You see, I'm a servant of the king, whether or not I realize it. I'm not the law unto myself. The King's word is final and carries all authority, and most of the time I wasn't even consulting Him about what He wanted me to do. Not so anymore. Perhaps, like me, you spent years striving and grinding but could not realize your full potential? I may have some insights for you. I was like an unbroken wild mustang who wouldn't allow anyone to ride or bridle him. Horses like that are essentially worthless for accomplishing any meaningful, productive work. Now consider the Clydesdale that's so powerful it can pull a house off its foundation but is still gentle enough to take a little child for a ride on his back - which one are you?

HAVE GREATER REVERENCE AND FEAR FOR THE CONSEQUENCES OF DISOBEDIENCE THAN YOU DO FOR DISAPPOINTING PEOPLE AROUND YOU

Our culture celebrates the "rebel without a cause" persona, but not the Kingdom. The King said that the meek shall inherit the Earth. My pastor used to describe meekness as power under control. It's about knowing the season, knowing the opportunity, and understanding the correct strategy and force required for the task at hand. That level of sensitivity and control requires moment-by-moment intimacy with Holy Spirit, deep reverence and fear for God, and full, unreserved obedience.

So work hard, but only at the things God is telling you to do. Don't slay dragons of your choosing because your intellect tells you it makes sense on paper, or because people are pushing you to do so. Have greater reverence and fear for the consequences of disobedience than you do for disappointing people around you, or the demands of your business, family, or your ministry. The fact is you will fear God, or you will fear man, and you will serve and submit to the one you fear and revere most. You choose.

If you're like me, you may have just had a somewhat somber moment of clarity. The weight of responsibility to obey God and work hard with fear and reverence is not wasted on kings. It's real and it should cause us all to pause and take a serious look at our calendars, our bank accounts, and relationships. Where you spend your time, money, and affections will help inform you if you've crashed through the guardrails of obedience and reverence for the King or not. Perhaps consider spending some time today asking God to speak to you about His mission and passion for you. Don't worry, it will likely reawaken dreams and passions that are already in you, the good works, prepared in advance for you to do.

> *Ephesians 2:10 (NAS): For we are His workmanship, created in Christ Jesus for good works, which God prepared beforehand so that we would walk in them..*

Let that moment sink in. And then read on.

Like the perfect, gracious Father that He is, God is also working (same word) in us to give us the desire and power to do what pleases Him. If life in the Kingdom has taught me one thing, it is that our King is far more committed to working on our behalf than we are committed to listening and seeking Him. So whatever level of seeking you're doing right now, make no mistake, He's speaking, guiding, leading, loving, and working for your good and breakthrough even more. Recall in John 15 Jesus calls his Father the "vinedresser" or in other translations "gardener".

> *John 15:1–2 (NAS): 1 "I am the true vine, and My Father is the vinedresser.*
>
> *2 "Every branch in Me that does not bear fruit, He takes away; and every branch that bears fruit, He prunes it so that it may bear more fruit.*

Notice that the vine and branches have very little responsibility in this process? The branch's nature is to remain connected to the vine, right? The vine is planted in the ground and both simply grow, and are trained, in response to the vinedresser's pruning, bending, and binding. He has the responsibility to manicure and direct the branches with tender expertise to bring about maximum fruitfulness. Pruning can be painful, but if we understand that we're in the hands of a competent gardener, then we can actually surrender control and relax. He who began this good work will be faithful to complete it. Our response is simply to abide, as Jesus articulates in the next few verses.

> *John 15:3–11 (NAS): You are already clean because of the word which I have spoken to you.*
>
> *4 "Abide in Me, and I in you. As the branch cannot bear fruit of itself unless it abides in the vine, so neither can you unless you abide in Me.*
>
> *5 "I am the vine, you are the branches; he who abides in Me and I in him, he bears much fruit, for apart from Me you can do nothing.*
>
> *6 "If anyone does not abide in Me, he is thrown away as a branch and dries up; and they gather them, and cast them into the fire and they are burned.*
>
> *7 "If you abide in Me, and My words abide in you, ask whatever you wish, and it will be done for you.*
>
> *8 "My Father is glorified by this, that you bear much fruit, and so prove to be My disciples.*
>
> *9 "Just as the Father has loved Me, I have also loved you; abide in My love.*
>
> *10 "If you keep My commandments, you will abide in My love; just as I have kept My Father's commandments and abide in His love.*
>
> *11 "These things I have spoken to you so that My joy may be in you, and that your joy may be made full.*

The secret to progress in this next season for Kings is to lean into Father God to seek His voice, His leading, His movements and let Him prune so we know where to pour out our energy to be fruitful. And in that beautiful context, He gives us the desires and the power to do the work that pleases Him, the bearing of much fruit that brings Him glory.

So while I feel the weight of responsibility to work hard with fear and reverence, I simultaneously feel filled with peace and confidence because of what He does to guide my growth, and to fuel my work as I abide in loving relational connection with Him. In this context, Jesus makes some absurdly awesome promises, and the Father is pleased to lavish His love on us. If you've felt the love of the Father, you know it doesn't get better than that.

My friend IBen describes this power and desire as "flow". It's as if God puts you on like a glove, and you have supernatural wisdom for the task at hand, energy and excitement about the work and the outcome, and you accomplish your work with greater speed and excellence than you could ever do on your own. Kings shine the brightest when functioning out of a place of abiding and it proves their salvation and connection to something or, more accurately, someone supernatural. It demonstrates what work looks like when the worker is connected to and informed by a third heaven relationship.

Conversely, we all know what it's like to grind and strive out of our own efforts apart from this desire and power. When we're not in sync with Holy Spirit, the work is often frustrating, fruitless, and lacks joy. It drains us and the outcome is often average. This is what life is like when you work hard serving *man*, and *not God.* It's the opposite of the passage below and it's the very thing your enemy is hoping you'll waste your whole life doing.

> *Colossians 3:23 (NAS): Whatever you do, do your work heartily, as for the Lord rather than for men,*

What if instead of being an unbreakable wild stallion, we put on the mindset of the beautiful and powerful Clydesdale, working hard

ONLY at the things that our King loves, watching Him multiply our efforts supernaturally while He provides resources, passion, and joy for the assignment, and the rest of the time we get to rest in His goodness? Could our new life in Christ really be that good?

But there's more... It's strange that Paul would say in the next verse that we should do everything without complaining or arguing, so we shine brightly in a world of crooked and perverse people, and so that no one can criticize us. Wow.... Those ideas seem totally unconnected to me at first, but consider this; what if that work that we're supposed to do, the work that God gives us a desire and power for, isn't the first thing we'd LIKE to do? What if this looks like service, surrender, putting others above ourselves, volunteering for the lowly work while we honor others?

You might think I've just contradicted myself from my previous thoughts, but let me explain.

Maybe you have become accustomed to doing the big picture vision work, the fun stuff, the work that's really in your "wheel-house" that fills you with energy and excitement. If so, that's great. I believe there is value in doing what God created you to do and if that means you're a visionary King, then by all means, do it with passion. Your family, organization, city, and ministry need you to do it well.

But is it possible that God may occasionally check the tenderness of our hearts, the sensitivity of our connection to Him by asking us to do something outside that scope? ...to clean toilets... to pick up garbage... to do your own administrative tasks or family chores? Maybe? Let me settle that one for you. The answer is YES!

And if this should happen, do everything without complaining or arguing. Don't argue or whine to Him and don't complain to others. That word "everything" in Greek means EVERYTHING. Sorry to break the news, my Kings. Your life is not your own and whining and complaining to those you lead isn't on the menu - ever. If you've got grievances, complaints, pain, then take it to your superior, Holy Spirit, and let Him instruct and comfort you. Take it to a carefully selected inner counsel who you know is for you and who will call you up, and not just enable and commiserate.

You'll notice as you cultivate a state of gratitude, joy, and perseverance in all circumstances - good or bad - that your influence and authority will grow as a King. And unfortunately, you'll also experience a negative impact on your leadership anointing if you grumble, complain, and argue. God's kings who are connected to His heart carry the most hope in every circumstance. This doesn't mean they're disconnected from their feelings, but it DOES mean they're not overwhelmed by them. They can hold in tension the painful emotions caused by difficult situations and simultaneously remain filled with the hope of glory and the salvation of God. In the midst of painful trials, they don't forget their identity, their citizenship, and their inheritance, instead they draw strength from them as they endure.

In God's Kingdom, commands like we learn from the above scripture are not designed to be a "try harder, do better" mandate for the sons and daughters of God to shoulder on our own. Let's be real. None of us has the natural ability to do EVERYTHING without complaining and arguing in our own strength. For all of us, there has to be an "X" factor if we are to accomplish this.

Jesus is our brother, firstborn among the dead, sacrificed and resurrected to reconnect us to God Himself. He is our model for what a truly Spirit-filled human being can do. And let's not forget the impossibly amazing Holy Spirit that has been sent down to indwell us with the same power that resurrected Jesus from the dead. We've been given the very mind of Christ Himself through the Holy Spirit. The Bible also says we have angelic hosts to help us.

This radical upgrade in our identity, mind, body, and spirit that occurred when we were born again is what prompted Paul to describe us as new "creatures", who've been reconciled to God through Jesus, and now we have a ministry that includes reconnecting others to God in the same way. See below.

> *2 Corinthians 5:17–18 (NAS): Therefore if anyone is in Christ, he is a new creature; the old things passed away; behold, new things have come.*
>
> *18 Now all these things are from God, who reconciled us to Himself through Christ and gave us the ministry of reconciliation,*

Kings, if you were still just a plain old human being, you could not fulfill the mission outlined in our Philippians passage, but because you're a new creature in Christ, this mission is definitely possible. Our directive has been imbued with divine resources, energy, power, wisdom, and anything else we need. And it comes with a promise that our light will shine bright in a perverse and crooked generation. Translation - your influence, visibility, authority, power, voice, will grow and stand out as distinct from others around you.

Again, we are discovering the process to bring Heaven to Earth for kings is a counterintuitive march away from control, self-preservation, and self promotion. It's a fierce pursuit that will test you. It's a supernatural partnership with Holy Spirit that will astonish you. It's surrendering to the hard work He's set before us walking in lock-step obedience with joy that's always available because of His presence.

Kings, this is what you were born for. Your life and presence will create an environment where your employees, friends, family, and others you lead and love will thrive. Even those perverse and crooked people that encounter you will acknowledge your God through your hard work. So get to it.

Chapter 4

EARTHQUAKE PRAISE PIT

Around midnight Paul and Silas were praying and singing hymns to God, and the other prisoners were listening. 26 Suddenly, there was a massive earthquake, and the prison was shaken to its foundations. All the doors immediately flew open, and the chains of every prisoner fell off! 27 The jailer woke up to see the prison doors wide open. He assumed the prisoners had escaped, so he drew his sword to kill himself. 28 But Paul shouted to him, "Stop! Don't kill yourself! We are all here!" 29 The jailer called for lights and ran to the dungeon and fell down trembling before Paul and Silas. 30 Then he brought them out and asked, "Sirs, what must I do to be saved?"

—ACTS 16:25–30 (NLT)

I wonder if Paul and Silas had ever discussed Jesus' promise of abundant life from John 10:10 with the other apostles. In that teaching, Jesus goes out of his way to draw a sharp contrast between what He is doing, and what the Devil is doing. The Devil's aim is to steal, kill, destroy. Jesus' mission is to bring full, abundant, overflowing life. I wonder if Paul and Silas ruminated on the real meaning of those words - from prison.

In other passages, Jesus says He came to free captives through salvation. Too often I can tend to over spiritualize Jesus' words and they lose their grasp on our practical day-to-day existence.

It's obvious that they were "free" spiritually, but in prison physically. Spiritual/physical dichotomy. Yet we know that the spiritual and physical realms are inexplicably intertwined and we are to manifest Heaven on Earth. Jesus didn't just walk around just preaching and pontificating like the religious leaders of His day. He DEMONSTRATED the supremacy of the spiritual realms over the physical via miracles, signs, and wonders. In my life, I've seen physical miracles, signs, and impossible, unexplainable wonders that confirm this reality.

In our little Midwest church, we saw people get healed from various illnesses, and given many additional years of healthy life after doctors declared they had only months to live. We saw legs grow out and even a resurrection from the dead all through Holy Spirit's manifested power as we worshipped and prayed as a unified body. We saw addicts healed and set free, many were born again, and individuals freed from demons. But there were also those who didn't get healed, who died, who didn't get free.

So what about this prison? Paul and Silas obviously tapped into a different Spiritual realm that afforded them the capacity for praise while physically trapped in a pit. It doesn't specify in the passage whether or not they were "feeling it". This is an important point for kings to consider. Maybe Paul and Silas were overwhelmed with the presence of the Holy Spirit so much that it made them overflow with praise and joy. Or maybe they knew the power of praise as a weapon and resolved to use it to defeat their spiritual enemy and rise above their circumstances - despite their discouragement and physical pain. Either way, they did it, presumably, out of obedience to Holy Spirit's prompting at that moment. God's kings grow in that kind of Spiritual connection and discernment through their commitment to abiding.

As we've explored, abiding is a simple, but difficult thing to master. The fact is, I'll never do it well unless I'm willing to take the risk, tackle the obstacle, face the fear, let go of control, and resolve in my mind how I'm going to show up when life unexpectedly blows up. On my best days, I'm here for it.

On my not-so-good days, I'm negotiating the terms of my surrender to God's will non-stop. I want the blessings of sonship; I want the authority; I want the intimacy, adventure, meaning and purpose. I want to tell my giant-killing stories to my kids. However, I want NONE of the hardships and challenges that are the prerequisites. I want to be an overcomer without fighting a battle. I want to be an obedient son without sacrificing anything. I don't want to give up money, time, friends, comforts, status, pleasures, possessions, or anything else that I currently cling to for security or have attached my affection to.

Like I said, abiding is really quite simple, but it can be quite difficult. Like you, I'm being refined and helped along this journey by Holy Spirit. A simple working definition of abiding is simply allowing Holy Spirit's words to influence your actions. Jesus' teaching on abiding is really simple - He's the vine, we're the branches, when we're disconnected from Him we can't produce fruit. As we learned earlier, you're positioned as a royal son, seated with Christ in the 3rd heaven. You're now the "house" that Holy Spirit lives in while He's here on Earth and He is speaking to you in a variety of ways - words, thoughts, feelings, scripture, this book, wise teachers and spiritual fathers, dreams, visions, and a host of other ways. Learning to abide is simply learning to hear His voice as He weaves these elements together into a unified narrative over and above the disjointed noise in our Earthly environment, the voices of our enemy, and the voice of our unrenewed intellect. As we move through this book, we'll unpack this in detail because abiding is a non-negotiable key for sons to carry the power and authority of our King and to represent His Kingdom well.

ON MY NOT-SO-GOOD DAYS, I'M NEGOTIATING THE TERMS OF MY SURRENDER TO GOD'S WILL NON-STOP.

It's a worthy and noble quest for a son and a king to pursue God at this level. To be sure, it will involve dying to yourself in ways you probably can't anticipate, but I'm convinced there's true joy on the other side of this journey. How else could someone sing praises from prison AND stay to save the jailer after they'd been freed! That's next-level joy, obedience, perseverance, sensitivity to Holy Spirit's voice and leading. But isn't that what we want in our heart of hearts? Don't we want to be kings that have full access to a power inside of us that is greater than any circumstance outside of us?

Reality is that kings don't get strong in the palace, we usually get lazy. Kings, you know what I'm talking about. If you're the exception to the rule, please send me a message so we can talk more about how you've avoided the singularly most effective trap in human history - comfort and complacency.

I get stronger in the gym, not on my couch. Don't forget, my physical man and spiritual man live in intertwined realms. We'd do well to take some obvious cues from the physical realm and accept the reality that to become giant killers, we need to spend some time in the spiritual gym. Like David, our lions and bears in the wilderness prepare us for a future fight. In the process, we discover who we are, discover who our God is, and learn how to remain connected to Him in the heat of battle.

The best stories will belong to those who stare the Devil in the face, take an inventory of the hopelessness, fear, and anguish of the moment, and then launch an assault of earthquake-level praise from the darkest pit anyway.

Today I pray God's grace over you if you have been lured into a trap of comfort or apathy. Good news, the fact that you're reading this book is proof of your desire to shift your life from complacency to action, from the shallows to the deep waters of abiding. Even if it's feels small, that's okay. Don't despise the day of small beginnings. God loves to see the work begin as much as He loves the eventual outcome. Below is a list to get you started. Let this be a launch point for conversation between you and Holy Spirit. The one that "leaps" off the page is likely the one He is speaking to you about. If none of them leap off the page, then ask Him to talk to you about what you should do and let Him guide your thoughts and imagination.

STEPS TO ABIDING

- work out
- read John 15
- spend the next several minutes in listening prayer
- get your wife flowers
- go for a drive and help a stranger
- serve your family by doing something the Holy Spirit prompts you to do
- do something you've been putting off
- have coffee with a trusted friend or mentor to process what you're learning from this book
- take communion
- take a nap
- worship while you work

You may find a few of the suggestions above "unspiritual". That's intentional. Kings need to break the overly spiritual paradigm that we've created around our relationship with our Heavenly Father and realize that Holy Spirit is speaking to us about both spiritual and physical things all the time. Remember, you're a new creation. You're presently seated in three intertwined physical and spiritual realms, so everything you do has impact in all three realms. Remember our simple definition of abiding, allowing the Holy Spirit to influence your actions. Holy Spirit is the third person of the Trinity. He knows that you have physical, spiritual, and relational needs and responsibilities. He doesn't speak to you only when you're having "quiet time" or in a church service. I've heard Him say all the above things to me at various times throughout the day because He knows what I need and His presence in my life is intensely practical.

I pray right now that Holy Spirit speaks a clear directive in your mind for one concrete step you can take right now toward abiding. You know what to do, kings. Let's roll.

Chapter 5

<< RE-WIND: PAUL'S ANGER MANAGEMENT PROBLEMS

I take so much solace in knowing that Bible people weren't perfect. I think we almost always read the scriptures through a subconscious filter that strips these characters of their real humanity. They don't get hungry; they don't poop; they don't get tired and for sure don't yell at people, tell lies, lust, commit adultery, masterbate, cheat, kill, etc. Even when we see them doing those things in black and white, we still somehow don't connect with their shared experiences of life.

This is dangerous because it makes the Bible, the people, and the stories inaccessible. It makes the pages irrelevant, as though we were reading fiction, and the wisdom hidden within seems inapplicable to circumstances we're going through. This subconscious filter makes a real relationship with God seem practically unattainable.

When we see Noah's drunkenness, or read how Abraham lied to the king of Egypt about Sarah, or when we see how Moses struck the rock instead of speaking to it, or recall David's adultery and murder, we somehow read past these massive failures and give them a "pass" because they're "Bible-people". Today, I was struck by the circumstances that landed Paul and Silas in jail. I've missed it for many years, but today it came alive.

> *Acts 16:16–24 (NLT):*
>
> *One day, as we were going down to the place of prayer, we met a slave girl who had a spirit that enabled her to tell the future. She earned a lot of money for her masters by telling fortunes. 17 She followed Paul and the rest of us, shouting, "These men are servants of the Most High God, and they have come to tell you how to be saved."*
>
> *18 This went on day after day until Paul got so exasperated that he turned and said to the demon within her, "I command you in the name of Jesus Christ to come out of her." And instantly it left her.*
>
> *19 Her masters' hopes of wealth were now shattered, so they grabbed Paul and Silas and dragged them before the authorities at the marketplace. 20 "The whole city is in an uproar because of these Jews!" they shouted to the city officials. 21 "They are teaching customs that are illegal for us Romans to practice."*
>
> *22 A mob quickly formed against Paul and Silas, and the city officials ordered them stripped and beaten with wooden rods. 23 They were severely beaten, and then they were thrown into prison. The jailer was ordered to make sure they didn't escape. 24 So the jailer put them into the inner dungeon and clamped their feet in the stocks.*

Did you catch that? Paul got "exasperated". There's so much going on in this passage that it's easy to miss this detail that Luke includes. But I'm glad he did because it gives us a window into Paul's humanity in that moment and as I meditated on this, I began to ask questions. Why didn't Paul heal and deliver her prior to this moment out of compassion? Was he being obedient to God and NOT healing her, just as Jesus said that He only does and says what He sees/hears His Father doing/saying? What was Holy Spirit saying to him about her in the moments leading up to this deliverance? Was he obeying or disobeying Holy Spirit? Was he arguing with Holy Spirit or trying to discern what to do, but having difficulty hearing well? Why would he allow this to go on to the point of exasperation? Did he know she was a money-maker for her owners and did he know that could escalate into a bigger problem for him if he healed her and disrupted their income? It must have been very disruptive to his preaching to be heckled in this way day after day.

HAVE YOU EVER SNAPPED? WHEN YOU DID, WHAT DID YOU DO? DID YOU PERFORM AN EXORCISM? NEITHER DID I.

Whatever the reason, he waits, and after a few days of this non-stop jeering from her, in exasperation, he snapped. And it's interesting that even though he was acting in frustration at that moment, he still carried the authority to cast out this demon.

Have you ever snapped? When you did, what did you do? Did you perform an exorcism? Neither did I. But Paul is a professional Christian, so when he snaps, he sets someone free from demonic oppression. But let's examine this for a moment. Is the Holy Spirit ever exasperated? No. But notice, the authority Paul had in the Spiritual realm over demons still functioned, even though he was not using that authority according to the Holy Spirit. Did I read that right? Paul "redlined" because of physical and mental exhaustion and transitioned out of peace, love, joy, patience, kindness, and goodness in the Spirit, to a place of tiredness, frustration, and exasperation in his flesh. Snap. All of us have been there. For me, it can occur many times per day. Perhaps I'm not the only one?

But God is so good, the authority Jesus paid for on the cross is still available to us, even in those moments. It's wild that God would allow imperfect vessels to carry His incredible power when we have the potential to wield it from a "fleshy" place.

But I believe, even in this demonstration of Heavenly power, Paul sows a seed and reaps a harvest. The seed was the expression of his frustration. He lost his temper. When we lose our temper, we're sowing seeds and we will not like what we reap. God allows a series of events to unfold after this that are really tough on Paul and Silas. An angry mob drags them before the Romans and they're falsely accused of crimes, beaten, and jailed.

While he was being beaten, I bet Paul was longing to rewind back to the point in the day where his worst problem was being heckled by an annoying servant girl. Before the jail cell worship service, I wonder if Silas had a few choice words for Paul about his temper and how it had landed them in a mess. Remember, they're REAL people.

Whatever conversations happened between them earlier in the day, they worked it out by midnight because the Bible says in Acts 16:25 (NLT): *"around midnight" Paul and Silas were praying and singing hymns to God..."*.

The good news is that within a few hours, Paul had a change of heart and perspective, and that's really the takeaway, right? He went from being exasperated by a minor annoyance, to singing and praising God in a literal prison. A lot happened in Paul's heart and mind from morning to midnight. His spirit and mind realigned with Heaven and he began manifesting fruit of the Spirit again, despite the fact that his circumstances went from annoying to horrible. Kings know the importance of alignment and rapid RE-alignment.

There are so many lessons in this for me, but let me summarize it this way. I'd suggest that God doesn't take away my authority when I allow my mind and flesh to rule, and abuse my authority out of a place of anger, fear, or any other unhealthy place. However, He will allow immediate and even possibly severe discipline to move me back into the safety of alignment and connection with Holy Spirit. This is because He needs His kings to represent His kingdom with self-control. And notice that after Paul's realignment, God was quick to break into their dire circumstances and perform an incredible miracle to deliver them from the mess they'd landed in. The real evidence of Paul's mindset shift is that he didn't run out of the jail to save his own skin - like I would have - instead he stays to show compassion to the jailer. Re-alignment with Holy Spirit will radically upgrade your behavior. Paul went from angry and annoyed over a relatively minor inconvenience to radically peaceful and powerful in a terrifying, life-threatening situation.

KINGS KNOW THE IMPORTANCE OF ALIGNMENT AND RAPID RE-ALIGNMENT.

I love Paul's rapid repentance and realignment with the Spirit. And I REALLY love to see how the Spirit responds. Was Paul perfect after this moment? No, but I believe it was a major milestone in his life where he probably resolved some things internally about his temper, and his Father's goodness, and the importance of abiding.

The power of Holy Spirit to break into your circumstances is not only real, it's your birthright as a son of God. If He did it for Paul and Silas, He'll do it for you. Remember, you're not stumbling through this life alone and the Bible is not a book of exceptions, it's a book of examples. You've got the Spirit that raised Christ from the dead, and He who formed the universe is living inside you. I declare to your Spirit right now - KING!! COME AWAKE TO YOUR NEW LIFE IN CHRIST! If you're doubting whether you really walk in power, if you doubt whether circumstances can abruptly change for you, if you've put yourself on spiritual probation or disqualified yourself from walking in your authority because you've made too many mistakes, then you've allowed a lie to take root in your mind. Stop. Re-align your thinking with the truth of Jesus' own words:

Matthew 19:26 (AMP): 26 But Jesus looked at them and said, With men this is impossible, but all things are possible with God. [Gen. 18:14; Job 42:2.]

We will never step into divine destiny if we don't align our thinking with our Heavenly reality. Any doubt, fear, or pessimism about a situation in your life is evidence that a lie is present and sabotaging your connection to your divine reality. Jesus paid for you to become reconnected to the higher reality of Heaven. Don't allow lies to undermine this truth! Don't misunderstand, I'm not saying everything always works out like some TV sitcom if we just believe correctly. I'm saying that no matter the outcome, our mindset is our choice and Holy Spirit's mission is to renew our mind so we can always take hold of the truth and detect and reject lies in EVERY situation. Whether or not the jail walls fell, Paul and Silas were worshipping. They had no guarantee that the walls would come down and that they would be set free. They probably hadn't even considered that as a possibility, but they were worshipping in the midst of the situation because they aligned their hearts and minds with Heaven, not Earth.

Abiding means you live with the ONGOING conviction that in any circumstance, Holy Spirit can break in, cause an earthquake, resurrect the dead, cast out the demon, heal the sick, and do whatever else is on God's agenda. As His king and ambassador of His kingdom, we have to believe in the supremacy of His power and His ability and eagerness to manifest the realities of Heaven on Earth. Your process for alignment into this reality may look like praise from a prison. I don't want to minimize the challenge in this. Kings, you will have to fight for this mindset. As you'll recall from earlier chapters, demons like Bitterness, Anger, Despair, Fear, and a host of others are right there in those moments, whispering their lies in your ear. Just as it was in the Garden of Eden, they'll appeal to your earthbound intellect, coach you to see the situation through their lenses of doubt and unbelief, and try to sever your lifeline to Holy Spirit's power and truth.

Their monologues can be so convincing. They make statements like: "This will never work...". "It didn't work out last time, it probably won't work out this time either." "You don't have enough talent or money or time for this." "No one else believes in you." "Don't pray for anything too radical. People will get freaked out or you'll set them up for disappointment when God doesn't show up." "God is punishing you and has abandoned you. You've made too many mistakes for God to do anything for you. You've prayed for years and nothing seems to happen. Give up."

You've probably heard all these lies in your head when facing difficult situations. Kings, we must be ruthless with these lies. I know they seem undeniable and true on the surface because they align with the Earthly circumstances you're facing. But we HAVE to listen to Holy Spirit give us the superior truth in these moments. We're citizens of Heaven, and foreigners on Earth. Heaven has total authority and dominion over Earth and all demonic powers and principalities in the unseen second realm. This means that at any moment our King may give you a command that originates in Heaven that has the power to alter your Earthly situation. Through intimacy with Holy Spirit, kings become masters at catching the superior truth in every situation and crushing the lies of the enemy to bring Heaven's reality into the Earth.

I leave you with the story of David and Goliath. Read this story and observe the lies the armies of Israel had believed that had completely sabotaged their power, courage, and will to fight. They were lost in fear, doubt, and unbelief. David was aligned with a superior truth, and had supernatural courage from a different Kingdom, and it made all the difference. Not only did God give them victory through David, but David's demonstration of power from Heaven infused power into the hearts of an entire army who shifted from fearful to ferocious. Their actions followed, and instead of continuing to cower at the thought of fighting the Philistines, they chased them and utterly destroyed them, plundered their camp, and gained an incredible victory. You know what to do, kings. Get control over your mind and take the thoughts of your enemy captive. Don't let the inferior reality of the problem you're facing here on Earth undermine your royal identity and power. Step up. Run to face your giant. All of Heaven is behind you and a growing army of brothers in arms is running alongside you.

1 Samuel 17:12–58 (NLT):

12 Now David was the son of a man named Jesse, an Ephrathite from Bethlehem in the land of Judah. Jesse was an old man at that time, and he had eight sons. 13 Jesse's three oldest sons—Eliab, Abinadab, and Shimea—had already joined Saul's army to fight the Philistines. 14 David was the youngest son. David's three oldest brothers stayed with Saul's army, 15 but David went back and forth so he could help his father with the sheep in Bethlehem.

16 For forty days, every morning and evening, the Philistine champion strutted in front of the Israelite army.

17 One day Jesse said to David, "Take this basket of roasted grain and these ten loaves of bread, and carry them quickly to your brothers. 18 And give these ten cuts of cheese to their captain. See how your brothers are getting along, and bring back a report on how they are doing." 19 David's brothers were with Saul and the Israelite army at the valley of Elah, fighting against the Philistines.

20 So David left the sheep with another shepherd and set out early the next morning with the gifts, as Jesse had directed him. He arrived at the camp just as the Israelite army was leaving for the battlefield with shouts and battle cries. 21 Soon the Israelite and Philistine forces stood facing each other, army against army. 22 David left his things with the keeper of supplies and hurried out to the ranks to greet his brothers. 23 As he was talking with them, Goliath, the Philistine champion from Gath, came out from the Philistine ranks. Then David heard him shout his usual taunt to the army of Israel.

24 As soon as the Israelite army saw him, they began to run away in fright. 25 "Have you seen the giant?" the men asked. "He comes out each day to defy Israel. The king has offered a huge reward to anyone who kills him. He will give that man one of his daughters for a wife, and the man's entire family will be exempted from paying taxes!"

26 David asked the soldiers standing nearby, "What will a man get for killing this Philistine and ending his defiance of Israel? Who is this pagan Philistine anyway, that he is allowed to defy the armies of the living God?"

27 And these men gave David the same reply. They said, "Yes, that is the reward for killing him."

28 But when David's oldest brother, Eliab, heard David talking to the men, he was angry. "What are you doing around here anyway?" he demanded. "What about those few sheep you're supposed to be taking care of? I know about your pride and deceit. You just want to see the battle!"

29 "What have I done now?" David replied. "I was only asking
a question!" 30 He walked over to some others and asked them
the same thing and received the same answer. 31 Then David's
question was reported to King Saul, and the king sent for him.

32 "Don't worry about this Philistine," David told Saul. "I'll go fight him!"

33 "Don't be ridiculous!" Saul replied. "There's no way you can fight this Philistine and possibly win! You're only a boy, and he's been a man of war since his youth."

34 But David persisted. "I have been taking care of my father's sheep
and goats," he said. "When a lion or a bear comes to steal a lamb
from the flock, 35 I go after it with a club and rescue the lamb from
its mouth. If the animal turns on me, I catch it by the jaw and club
it to death. 36 I have done this to both lions and bears, and I'll do it
to this pagan Philistine, too, for he has defied the armies of the living
God! 37 The Lord who rescued me from the claws of the lion and the
bear will rescue me from this Philistine!"

Saul finally consented. "All right, go ahead," he said. "And may the Lord be with you!"

38 Then Saul gave David his own armor—a bronze helmet and a coat of mail. 39 David put it on, strapped the sword over it, and took a step or two to see what it was like, for he had never worn such things before.

"I can't go in these," he protested to Saul. "I'm not used to them." So David took them off again. 40 He picked up five smooth stones from a stream and put them into his shepherd's bag. Then, armed only with his shepherd's staff and sling, he started across the valley to fight the Philistine.

41 Goliath walked out toward David with his shield bearer ahead of him, 42 sneering in contempt at this ruddy-faced boy. 43 "Am I a dog," he roared at David, "that you come at me with a stick?" And he cursed David by the names of his gods. 44 "Come over here, and I'll give your flesh to the birds and wild animals!" Goliath yelled.

45 David replied to the Philistine, "You come to me with sword, spear, and javelin, but I come to you in the name of the Lord of Heaven's Armies—the God of the armies of Israel, whom you have defied. 46 Today the Lord will conquer you, and I will kill you and cut off your head. And then I will give the dead bodies of your men to the birds and wild animals, and the whole world will know that there is a God in Israel! 47 And everyone assembled here will know that the Lord rescues his people, but not with sword and spear. This is the Lord's battle, and he will give you to us!"

48 As Goliath moved closer to attack, David quickly ran out to meet him. 49 Reaching into his shepherd's bag and taking out a stone, he hurled it with his sling and hit the Philistine in the forehead. The stone sank in, and Goliath stumbled and fell face down on the ground.

50 So David triumphed over the Philistine with only a sling and a stone, for he had no sword. 51 Then David ran over and pulled Goliath's sword from its sheath. David used it to kill him and cut off his head.

Israel Routs the Philistines

When the Philistines saw that their champion was dead, they turned and ran. 52 Then the men of Israel and Judah gave a great shout of triumph and rushed after the Philistines, chasing them as far as Gath and the gates of Ekron. The bodies of the dead and wounded Philistines were strewn all along the road from Shaaraim, as far as Gath and Ekron. 53 Then the Israelite army returned and plundered the deserted Philistine camp. 54 (David took the Philistine's head to Jerusalem, but he stored the man's armor in his own tent.)

55 As Saul watched David go out to fight the Philistine, he asked Abner, the commander of his army, "Abner, whose son is this young man?"

"I really don't know," Abner declared.

56 "Well, find out who he is!" the king told him.

57 As soon as David returned from killing Goliath, Abner brought him to Saul with the Philistine's head still in his hand. 58 "Tell me about your father, young man," Saul said.

And David replied, "His name is Jesse, and we live in Bethlehem."

Chapter 6

GOLIATH IS HOLDING YOUR SWORD

As a rule, I doubt most of us have fought and defeated bears and lions in the wilderness when no one was watching. We've not dedicated the bulk of our lives to being a living offering of praise under the stars while diligently caring for our father's possessions. If you're like me, you probably started your adult life filled with ambition about the degree or job you would get, the wife you would win, and the track to success you would pave. It takes many forms, but it usually looks something like this: step 1) educate yourself with information to execute your plan. 2) insulate yourself from as much pain, work, risk and loss as possible, step 3) manipulate circumstances and people to your advantage to gain status, power, wealth. In short, climb ladders, promote your agenda, leverage your strengths to get what you desire. Network, move, shake, hustle and grind. Play the game and win. And if/when it works out well for us, we believe this represents the favor of God and all our methods that brought us here are validated. This has become such a part of our way of life that I honestly believe we do it on a subconscious level because it's hard-wired into us by our culture from birth. If you think you DON'T do this, let me ask you a question. The last time you were in the room with a "big" person, perhaps a successful businessman or woman, a famous person, etc., did you act or behave differently? Did you swoon? Did you get their autograph, or angle for a chance to talk to them? Did you attempt to sit by them, or get their attention with a pithy comment, or try to impress them in any way? Did you observe their needs above the needs of others in the room? Perhaps look past the wait staff, or others who you deemed less important?

I'm not saying it's wrong to honor people who are highly anointed or to acknowledge people who have been successful, or who are wise and gifted. I think this is absolutely right. But there is a very fine line between honor for their sake, and manipulation for OUR sake. These people are not gatekeepers to your destiny, and they're not pawns to be used and manipulated in a pretentious relationship to advance your agenda. Sometimes, to check my own motives in moments where I'm honored to be in the presence of "big" people, I'll intentionally and actively NOT seek to connect with them and instead pursue others in the room. I've found a lot of freedom in walking in the reality that I'm already known, loved, and promoted by the greatest and most incredible person to walk the planet, Jesus Christ, and I'm loved and adopted by His father, and I'm resourced in every way by the Holy Spirit. Talk about an incredible entourage! Kings, you need not posture and self-promote. God sets your appointments, assignments, and has established your value.

David is one of my favorite examples of this whole-hearted and innocent posture before God. He did not seek promotion, or attempt to network his way into favor and is described in scripture as a man after God's heart. Wholeheartedly, David pursued God, worshipped Him, and honored his assignment to protect a few sheep. He even risked his own life to fight off bears and lions just to save a few sheep. He did this with no illusion that he'd ever be anything more than the rejected runt of Jesse's house, who was a bit of an embarrassment because his mother was one of Jesse's servant girls. He must have known what his lot in life was going to be. He had no prospects, no upward economic or social mobility and probably no aspirations of advancement to speak of. His low standing was revealed by the fact that his father didn't bother to bring him in from the wilderness when the world's most famous prophet, Samuel, came over for dinner. All the other brothers were likely groomed and prepared for this extravagant event. David was left literally out in the cold. With no guarantees, or possibly even a hope of advancement, he simply leaned into his situation and resolved that God was his great reward. Under the stars, he worshipped his guts out and cultivated a relationship with God in his Spirit that was otherworldly. His internal world was the only thing he could manage, so that's what he did. God is looking for that kind of person to carry His mantle of leadership and authority.

In the Kingdom, promotion, leadership, and authority look a lot different. The world's value system makes accomplishment and achievement prerequisites for promotion. God's equation for promotion is: if you're faithful with little, you'll be given much. Steadfastness and perseverance in faith during seasons of testing and trial are higher on God's list of qualifications than the accolades of men or earthly achievement. He's looking at heart-level, internal character quality, and doesn't care so much about externals or flash. In the Kingdom, David is not the exception. He is the rule, along with other heroes of our faith, like Abraham, Joseph, the disciples, the apostles, and even Jesus, who was but a humble carpenter's son.

Plucked from obscurity - literally called in out of the fields, David is anointed King of Israel by Samuel, and then goes into the palace and leads a charmed life of luxury, power, wealth, and ease where he governs Israel into health, wealth, prosperity, and peace until he dies. Not quite. Actually, he goes back to tending sheep. He goes back to his secret wilderness to live life with God, his only intimate friend, to learn the ways of kingship. Later, we even see a recurring reluctance in David to take his place as king- a hallmark sign of a true king's heart.

David was qualified to be king because he cultivated a relational, intimate connection with God as his singular source of life and meaning, not because of his skill or pedigree. His success in the process of just "being" with God, every day, gave him the Spiritual sensitivity to know when the Spirit was empowering him to do supernatural and heroic feats and he felt that on the day he encountered Goliath.

The story tells us that Goliath's spear was huge, and his sword was amazingly crafted. With a single divinely guided stone released from the skillfully wielded sling of a wholehearted boy, a giant falls. Goliath presented the invitation for David to come out and lay claim to his authority. King Saul gave David his blessing to fight, and the Holy Spirit took the giant down using David's sling. At that moment a sling got upgraded to a sword, and a boy took up the mantle of king. His faithfulness was rewarded with divine authority.

DAVID WAS QUALIFIED TO BE KING BECAUSE HE CULTIVATED A RELATIONAL, INTIMATE CONNECTION WITH GOD AS HIS SINGULAR SOURCE OF LIFE AND MEANING, NOT BECAUSE OF HIS SKILL OR PEDIGREE.

We all love the idea of getting the upgrade. We don't love the process required to get the upgrade. We've been convinced it's too slow, too much work, too painful. The path is not linear, and it often makes no logical sense. After all, how does a shepherd boy become a king by tending his father's sheep in the wilderness, totally hidden from view? We grow tired of repeatedly explaining our decisions to well-intended but worldly minded brothers and sisters who question the sanity of our choices in seasons where we struggle and wander.

But manipulating your circumstances for peace, advancement, and progress is not the King's ultimate objective for his kings. Pulling down grace that overwhelms your circumstances is your inheritance. Connecting deeply with your King of Kings your path to defeating giants in your land and He has already mapped out the training program, the assignments, the promotions, and the upgrades HE wants you to have.

Ephesians says we're seated in Heavenly realms with Christ, but what in the heck does this really mean? Are there storms in Heaven? Are there any illnesses or wars or circumstances in Heaven that oppose us? Is Heaven in short supply of grace, peace, power, love, money, gold, strategies, answers, wisdom, joy, patience, etc.???

Obviously, you get the idea. But here's the reality - we actually DON'T get the idea. We read past these key scriptures that unlock our inheritance because a spirit of religion has inoculated us from their impact. Over generations, this religious spirit has infiltrated the Church with intellectualism, producing a hybrid spirituality that attempts to merge human logic with Kingdom wisdom. This hybrid wisdom has replaced the Heavenly mindset that "all things are possible" with an earthbound pragmatism that reduces our theology to our experiences and our pathway to promotion has become based on skill sets and networking. In this context, it has become normal to read Biblical stories of Jesus opening blind eyes, David defeating Goliath, or Paul's sweatband and Peter's shadow healing the sick, and assume that they must have been superhuman and not ordinary men. If this is our default, then we can easily shrug off any responsibility we have to emulate these same signs, miracles, and wonders in our own lives. Instead, we strategize and execute the plans of mere men, rather than carry out the assignments and exercise the authority of our King.

There is a false wisdom that lures God's kings to play it safe and build the most comfortable life you can on Earth. To live out your days in ease til you retire and die. But our King has modeled a different way, and instructed us to follow Him; to believe for things beyond our skills or abilities, to liberate captives, raise the dead, and command storms to be still. The older I get, the more I believe that we can't have both.

We will either throw out half of Scripture to pursue a life well within our skill set and comfort, or we will throw out the spirit of religion and pursue the Kingdom. This hybrid spirituality that masquerades as wisdom is a recycled, worldly, self-help gospel devoid of power. It puts the responsibility on you to build your life, rather than abide in Christ, and walk in Holy Spirit's power. The evidence speaks for itself. There is a conspicuous lack of signs, miracles, wonders, love, joy, peace, kindness, faithfulness, and self-control in our world, and sadly, in our churches as well. But I'm anchored to a promise from Jesus that through abiding in Him, we'll do the same, and even greater things than He did.

I believe we're living in the days of Gideon. We're living in the days where many unlikely heroes, currently hiding because they feel unqualified to lead, are going to receive visitations and calls to move out of their comfort zones to do exploits they could never accomplish on their own or take any credit for. It's a beautiful era to be living in - the era of glorious nobodies. The God of the universe is moving His Kingdom forward and supernaturally empowering some of the least competent, weakest, most unqualified people. Why?

WE WILL EITHER THROW OUT HALF OF SCRIPTURE TO PURSUE A LIFE WELL WITHIN OUR SKILL SET AND COMFORT, OR WE WILL THROW OUT THE SPIRIT OF RELIGION AND PURSUE THE KINGDOM.

I'd like to suggest a couple of reasons. But first some context. As we've discussed previously, our enemy is asserting his authority in the 1st and 2nd realms and unfortunately he has his hands on most of the control levers for the systems of this Earth. Whether it's the financial system, family, education, entertainment, business, politics, food, power, or even the church, there are hardly any arenas of life where his overt, evil influence can not be felt. However, spirit-filled believers have been given authority over him in every way and our mandate is to declare the kingdom of God is here and show the supremacy of God's kingdom over everything.

When God moves and His power is displayed, we are drawn to it. However, our history with powerful moves of God in the Church has taught us that if we're not careful; pride, jealousy, control, apathy, and many other demonic influences can sabotage us. What is our King's practical solution for this? I believe we can take our cues from stories of "heroes" like Gideon.

> **STEP 1** | Use someone who has no grid for pride, no cause for self-righteousness, self-promotion or selfish ambition. Choose a humble vessel.

> **STEP 2** | Test his heart and obedience by having him do a few unorthodox "warm-ups". For Gideon, this looked like going down into the camp of the enemy to receive a word from the Lord regarding the battle.

> **STEP 3** | Make that word cryptic and almost nonsensical - i.e. "round loaf of bread" etc. See how he responds when all his logic and rationale are frustrated. Will he still obey?

> **STEP 4** | Gather all the able-bodied men who can fight, then send ⅔ home.... further frustrating his logic.

> **STEP 5** | Send more men home until he's left with only a fraction of the original number, and definitely not enough to defeat the opposing army by the numbers... providing him more than ample cause for worry, panic, fear, and disorientation.

> **STEP 6** | Take away the swords and give the army trumpets and pots... to add another layer of absurdity to an already illogical strategy.

> **STEP 7** | Give instructions on exactly what to declare over the situation
>
> **STEP 8** | Win the battle

Kings, I believe this is our Heavenly Father's model for leadership development to train His kings to steward his glory as He ushers in a new era of revival on the Earth. He's raising up leaders in an unorthodox way and He's not inclined to change it because it frustrates our intellect, our institutions and our methods. Honestly, that's precisely the point. I believe we are living at a transitional moment in culture that is reminiscent of what Jesus stepped into as He introduced the Kingdom of Heaven to the Pharisees of his day. Jesus selected a ragtag bunch of fishermen and a few women to be His entourage and core group of followers and they utterly and unapologetically frustrated the methods and power structure of institutional religion and its leaders to the point of embarrassment.

If we crafted a battle strategy through analysis and logic, and hand-picked an elite team of spiritual operators to execute that strategy based on skills and abilities under the current cultural norms; we would NEVER come up with THIS plan, or THIS team. God likes it that way for a few reasons.

- It's totally impossible for any man to take credit for the resulting victory
- Because it's impossible for anyone to take credit, it's impossible for the victors to hold any grudge against those who didn't "fight". The ones who carried God's glory and received a great victory as a gift from God are to welcome and celebrate ALL those who come in after the fact with grace and humility, not with an arrogant grudge, as we can often be inclined to do.

- Through a few who were not afraid, the nation was restored. God loves people, and He REALLY loves saving them in grand and magnificent displays of His power. He's totally willing to bless an entire household because of one person who surrenders to Him. He'll bless a whole city if there are a few spirit-filled kings who remain faithful and honor Him there. And He'll deliver an entire nation through epic victories if just a few fearless warriors will obey - even if the strategy and methods make no logical sense.

It's your call. You can climb ladders, leverage skill sets, pass your coursework, maybe even wow people with your charisma and build your own empire. Or, you can partner with Holy Spirit to build our King's Kingdom and watch Him do immeasurably more than you could ask or imagine according to His power that is at work within us. If you build your own empire, then the stress of maintaining it is on you. If we build His Kingdom, then He is faithful to complete the work in and through us.

As King Saul discovered, your skills, credentials, anointing, and charisma won't help when you're toe to toe with a real Goliath, taunting and snarling at you, eager to take you out. That moment reveals the genuine kings and the impostors. Which one are you today? More importantly, which one are you going to be tomorrow and the next day? To be a real king, start by resolving to cultivate an intimacy with your Father and embrace His process for your training promotion - no matter how weird and countercultural it may be. Whether you're hiding in a winepress, or faithfully protecting a few sheep in the wilderness with a slingshot, remember that God is training you for victory in your future assignment. It's likely that your next promotion is in the hands of your next giant. Goliath is holding your sword, and when you're ready, Holy Spirit will help you take it. Until then, abide, and keep on training.

Chapter 7

THE CAT TURD THAT BROKE THE CAMEL'S BACK

I remember the night with crystal clarity. It had been a VERY frustrating day in a long line of frustrating days. I own a business and earlier in the day I'd learned that one of our newest, and largest, customers had received a shipment of damaged goods and we were going to have to replace them. Given that these products were custom made to order, this was going to cause tremendous expense and significant delay. What's the big deal? Stuff gets damaged in shipping all the time, right? Why let your feathers get so ruffled you ask? Let me provide some context. This news came on the heels of a long run of production challenges that stem from workmanship defects, poor QC, and packaging practices by our manufacturer. These habitual offenses had delayed receipt of a large purchase order from said customer. In fact, at this point we had been waiting for a few very large purchase orders to come in from this very large customer for a very long time, which had put our company and our family under great financial stress. Like - laying hands on food in the pantry and asking Holy Spirit to multiply it - level stress.

In addition, we had recently moved to a new city FAR away from our home in the Midwest, had left ministry, friends, family, homes and the security of jobs - all because the Holy Spirit appeared to us in a dream and said, "Go".

Oh, and this all occurred during a global pandemic that forced us into mandatory quarantines, remote schooling, church lock downs, political rage over maskers, anti-maskers, vaxxers, anti-vaxxers, etc. Yeah, good times. The environment was volatile to say the least, no I mean really volatile, as in, on fire, literally.

To add to the general mayhem, Northern California added its own special "sauce" to the chaotic recipe by being the epicenter of the two consecutive years of record setting forest fires, which gave us weeks on end of neuro-toxin level air pollution. Ash rained down on our cars and week after week the sun looked like something out of a Star Wars movie as it crossed the smoke filled sky. There was literally a point when we could drive 30 minutes in almost any direction and be on the front lines of a massively devastating fire.

To say people were on edge was an understatement. People wandered around like zombies with perpetual PTSD that could be triggered at any moment if they heard a siren, saw a cloud in the sky that looked like smoke or ran into someone at Costco without a mask on. Many people were barely holding onto their sanity, my family included.

It was on this special evening, after this long day, during this stressful personal and professional season, in this very volatile and chaotic time in our state, nation, and world, that my daughter's cat decided to defecate on my bed, which I discovered as I prepared to drift off to sleep and forget the worries, conflicts, stress and disappointments of the day.

In that season I vividly recall that my wife of 18 years, whom I love with all my heart, and I were barely holding it together, and both weary of fighting back the temptation to red-line at any moment. Our kids felt the pressure as we navigated this season of challenges and growth together as a family despite our attempts to keep their spirits buoyed and to keep the home environment light-hearted.

Needless to say, I didn't need the cat to shit on my bed. Let's just say it was the cherry on top of the giant crap sandwich we'd been munching for months and, despite my best efforts to control my temper, I completely lost it.

It's so easy to TALK about peace that passes understanding. It's so easy to envision how mature I am, and how strong I will be in a challenging situation. Then an opportunity to assert my strength and be mature comes and I let loose a string of profanity, yell at everyone within proximity, grab my keys, and stomp out of the house and drive down the 5 for about an hour toward nowhere before I finally turn around. Instead of showing up as the noble king I'd hoped to be, I popped off like a hot-headed teenage punk and brought shame to the family name.

During my anger-fueled drive, my internal monologue got pretty dark. I recited to God all the reasons this season sucks. I complained about my kids, wife, business, church, state politics, national politics, finances, COVID, wildfires, and pretty much everything that came to mind. Amid my whining, I am sad to say; I entertained some pretty dark thoughts.

At some point during the drive, a small voice broke in and said something like, "... you know these thoughts are not mine, and they're not yours, they are from your enemy... he wants to hurt you. I'm here for you when you want to talk..."

Thank you, Holy Spirit, for your kindness to me in the midst of my hostility and stupidity. If a cat turd can send me over the edge, how am I going to handle the more significant issues of kingship that are undoubtedly waiting for me as I grow into greater responsibility and authority? Yikes, I have so much to learn!

So I turned around. I put on worship music in my truck, and with all the faith and strength of a dead fish, I started singing, worshipping, and confessing with my mouth that Jesus is Lord. I rebuked the devil for his stupid thoughts. I revoked his authority, declared his attacks nullified, and consciously reattached my affection and hope to a higher Kingdom and my true reality. As I realigned my thinking with my King's, I actually chuckled to myself as I rolled back into my driveway. Ah... release...

I wish I could say everything resolved itself as I strode back into the house like a perfect sitcom. It didn't, and that's the point, right? Circumstances may be painful, finances might be a mess, health might fail, and relationships might be crumbling. The real question is, can I sleep at the bottom of the boat in the storm, or am I going to freak out? How long am I going to freak out? How many people am I going to hurt during my freak-out? How long before I realign with Holy Spirit, my identity, my role, and my King? How much of a mess am I going to have to clean up because of my freak-out? How quick am I going to repent, ask forgiveness, and get back in the game?

I REVOKED HIS AUTHORITY, DECLARED HIS ATTACKS NULLIFIED, AND CONSCIOUSLY REATTACHED MY AFFECTION AND HOPE TO A HIGHER KINGDOM AND MY TRUE REALITY.

These are questions kings ask themselves and need to answer honestly. I'm resolved to show up better next time. I'm glad to report that I was able to become a "better" version of myself in about an hour. That's progress. In the past, it could have been days. I was still tired and somewhat numb when I got home, but at least I wasn't swearing and seeking a cat to punt across the room - that's a win. Holy Spirit strode in the door ahead of me, generously pouring out grace for me, my daughter, my wife, even the cat.

In these moments, I can be tempted to go overboard on inward reflection that morphs into unproductive navel gazing. While that may be helpful for a short season, it can easily become a trap that leads to self-condemnation. My humble advice? Kings, don't give into this temptation when you hit the wall and discover you're not made of tougher stuff.

Consider these moments an opportunity to go to the Lord and let Him know you've officially reached your red-line limit and receive His grace. Jesus says my yoke is easy and my burden is light. Take His yoke and learn from Him in these moments, for He is meek and lowly in heart and you will find rest for your soul.

IF YOUR FAITH DOESN'T WORK WHEN YOU'RE IN THE PIT, THEN WHAT GOOD IS IT ON THE MOUNTAIN TOP?

> *Matthew 11:28–30 (NLT): Then Jesus said, "Come to me, all of you who are weary and carry heavy burdens, and I will give you rest. 29 Take my yoke upon you. Let me teach you, because I am humble and gentle at heart, and you will find rest for your souls. 30 For my yoke is easy to bear, and the burden I give you is light."*

Make no mistake, our King is so good that He allows circumstances like this to reveal our limits so that once we have them in crystal clear focus, He can reveal His power and goodness towards us. That's both the process and the point. This process is necessary because without it, our faith is just a bumper sticker slogan that's not really helpful when the shit hits the fan, or in my case, the bed. If your faith doesn't work when you're in the pit, then what good is it on the mountain top?

Jesus is uncompromising on this one fact: intimacy with Him as your source of strength for everything. If you think you're going to spend 12 hours a day at work and only 20 minutes a day with Him in the morning, think again. That's not a recipe for building spiritual muscle, and don't be surprised when you crumble under the weight of the world's "yoke" of stress and chaos. Remember, we were meant for fellowship with Him - unbroken, sustained, ongoing, continuous, and intimate. If we don't figure that out then I'd suggest we'll never fully walk in our inheritance of abundant, victorious life and our ability to manifest the love, joy, peace, patience, kindness, goodness, and self-control will be severely limited.

I'm not suggesting it's about our effort and striving to achieve super-spiritual status in the Kingdom. This isn't about logging more minutes of quiet time or trying harder - it's about abiding - whatever that looks like. It's relational, not formulaic. I am suggesting that we reap what we sow. If we invest our time, money, passion, energy and resources in a world set up against us, then we'll waste our life in a perpetual stress-filled and hopeless cycle that leads to death. However, if we pour into our relationship with our Creator, Savior, and Best Friend, and we pursue the Kingdom designed for us and resourced with all the power we will ever need, we'll reap abundant life better than we could ever dream.

Breaking point moments reveal where we are in the process, and invite us to regain focus.

> *Romans 8:18–22 (NLT): 18 Yet what we suffer now is nothing compared to the glory he will reveal to us later. 19 For all creation is waiting eagerly for that future day when God will reveal who his children really are. 20 Against its will, all creation was subjected to God's curse. But with eager hope, 21 the creation looks forward to the day when it will join God's children in glorious freedom from death and decay. 22 For we know that all creation has been groaning as in the pains of childbirth right up to the present time.*

While they're not perfect, kings always return to one central truth. That while we may face loneliness, financial ruin, crippling debt, challenges within work or business, lack, fear, doubt, Covid, relational stress, parenthood, forest fires, sickness, isolation, etc., we believe that these light and momentary afflictions are not worth comparing to the glory that will be revealed through us in this age AND in the age to come. We know that what we do to remain faithful in secret will eventually be rewarded openly.

We know our King is up to something and we're not abandoned, instead we're being groomed for something amazing. We know He's doing a deep and necessary work because this world that He loves needs to SEE how His kings show up and demonstrate the peace and power of His Kingdom. We are born to shine brightest in the darkest circumstances.

Heavenly Father, help us function in intimacy with you as our number one priority. Let your Kingdom be built in us first as we experience unbroken fellowship and friendship with you. Give us wisdom to know how to wield the weapons of our warfare to defend ourselves and our kingdoms from Satan's attacks and strategies. Let us not elevate any goal or mission above simply being your sons. Preserve us, sustain us, give us today our daily bread, and purify our hearts so that we seek you with our WHOLE heart. See that our affections and loyalties are not divided. Let us come into your presence and worship. Let us be filled as we take a drink from your well that never runs dry and let us never thirst again. Let us discover the "art" of abiding in you, remaining connected like the branches to the vine, so that we can live in your light, receive the nutrients our spirits need, and bear fruit according to your will. Purge from our minds all fear, doubt, pride, distraction, and all other things that are not from you, and replace them with the goodness and blessings of Heaven so that we are drenched in the fragrant oil of your goodness and the aroma of Heaven accompanies us everywhere we go. Amen.

Chapter 8

MAKE IT HURT

As we discovered in the previous chapter, trials, and even cat turds, reveal the truth about a person in a way that nothing else can. For example, I would never have known the degree to which I had allowed finances to dominate my life and define my self-worth without the trial of losing my job and bootstrapping a startup business with little to no income for two years. I would never have known how much my peace was connected to my control of my circumstances without the disruptive and painful challenge of COVID. I would never have learned how dependent I was on the praise and affirmation of my family and peers unless I'd moved away, against all their wishes. I wouldn't have known how much I lacked intimacy with my King without the isolation of the wilderness seasons in my life.

Dying to yourself is a hard process. Coming face to face with your weakness is messy and painful. If you're like me during those prolonged difficult seasons when you're stuck between mountain tops, you may be prone to outbursts of anger or sadness. You may even lament that God has abandoned you and have deep doubts about your faith. If this resonates with you, I want you to know that there is no shame or blame in this. We can all be quite whiny and weak in the trials and valleys of life. These valleys expose things we'd rather keep hidden, and reveal what you're made of - good or bad - in ways that nothing else can. Psalms, Lamentations, and Job all highlight the raw and profound way we humans respond in painful seasons. It's okay, God can take it. Give yourself permission to lament. If pain is in your heart, you must let it out. He knows it's there and wants to heal it. Trying to hide your fears, frustrations, disappointments is NOT permissible in the Kingdom just like concealing cancer is not an effective treatment, it's actually a death sentence.

I read these hard Scriptures, and even hear modern day stories of saints who've sacrificed so much for the Gospel and for our King, and I'm humbled by the flimsiness of my strength to face trials, to endure, and stay in peace. I take solace in the tone and authenticity of Job and David's responses to painful situations. Like them, we're not always cool under pressure and it's cathartic to express great sorrow and agony from your "valley" floor. It could be the key to lighting the pathway to your next mountain top.

A practical tactic I find helpful to gain perspective in these moments is simply acknowledging that it could always be worse. It's not super spiritual, but it is the truth. However, if I dwell there, I can pivot to shame over the fact that I should be stronger, I should be farther along, more mature, etc., and none of those thoughts are from God. Holy conviction in this moment simply serves to make us aware of our limitations, nothing more. If a cat turd causes you to red-line, then that's your limit. The point is to admit it, and make peace with it, draw close to Him, receive His strength in our weakness, and grow. Perhaps next time we'll have the grace to laugh at the cat turd instead of throwing a tantrum. Even Paul had thorns in his side that he pleaded with God to remove. But God's response was:

> *2 Corinthians 12:9 (NAS): And He has said to me, "My grace is sufficient for you, for power is perfected in weakness." Most gladly, therefore, I will rather boast about my weaknesses, so that the power of Christ may dwell in me.*

You're human, and your trials are very contextual to your life. God doesn't have crazy expectations about your "performance" in these seasons like you do. He has grace. He is far more patient with you than you are with yourself - I promise you. His desire is not that you dig in, try harder, and do better. His goal is to break the backbone of performance, religion, and shame by allowing you to get real in your weakness so He can become your strength. Only then can we fully receive His grace to endure and His power can be perfectly revealed in and through us.

Perhaps you've gone several rounds with a physical illness that's wreaked havoc on your life, or experienced the untimely death of a loved one, a bankruptcy, a loss of a job, a failed marriage. These trials test us and shake us to our very core.

TRYING TO HIDE YOUR FEARS, FRUSTRATIONS, DISAPPOINTMENTS IS NOT PERMISSIBLE IN THE KINGDOM JUST LIKE CONCEALING CANCER IS NOT AN EFFECTIVE TREATMENT, IT'S ACTUALLY A DEATH SENTENCE.

First, let me say that I don't believe God causes pain in our lives to punish us. If He does this, then that means that the cross of Christ didn't satisfy God's wrath and Jesus' sacrifice did not meet the requirement for judgment and justice for humanity's sin. But we know that it did, once and for all. Jesus himself confirms this with his final words as a "normal" human being when he said, "It is finished."

Let's get some context. Under the old covenant law, the punishment that humans deserved because of their sin was transferred onto an animal and that animal would be sacrificed to pay for that person's sin. Under the new covenant, Jesus became the perfect, final sacrifice required to satisfy God's justice as a payment for our sin for all time. No more animal sacrifice required under our new covenant. This is a massive shift from the religious obligations and religious system of the old covenant and into a new covenant of grace and relationship with Jesus. So, to be clear, the fiery, angry God of the Old Testament is not "mad" at us anymore because of our sin. He's dealt with sin once and for all when He poured all his wrath on Jesus instead of us. We are now the objects of His affection and members of His family, just like Jesus. By His own standard of perfection and justice, it is impossible for Him to punish a human who has put their faith in Jesus because we have been given perfect righteousness as a gift. There's literally nothing left to punish us for. We are viewed by all of Heaven as faultless, righteous, and holy.

It's critical to internalize this reality if you're going to see trials in their proper context, and embrace the hope that they will ALWAYS produce glorious fruit in our lives, despite the pain they cause. They are not punishment any more than our daily physical workout is punishment. Just like a physical workout reveals our physical limits; trials reveal our spiritual character and strengthen us so that we can carry the heavy mantle of authority God wants to put on us as His kings. And because the Earth is broken, the whole spectrum of our lives provides ample opportunities for character growth and development, because trials are literally everywhere.

Let me acknowledge I realize some of you have experienced unthinkable challenges and devastating loss in ways I could never imagine. I want you to know that I honor you and I do not make light of your pain and loss. In no way do I compare my frivolous inconvenience with my daughter's cat to the devastation of losing a child, a home, your health, a bankruptcy, or a marriage. My hope is that together we can frame up these seasons and events with Kingdom perspective and understand our Father's desire to flip the script on our enemy. If we can use our enemy's schemes against him to gain power, authority, joy, and advance the Kingdom, then that is the ultimate victory. This is what it means to be an overcomer, and MORE than a conqueror. This is not easy, and the pain of trials is very real. But kings, we have a hope that the world does not have that becomes our promise no matter how difficult the circumstances.

Romans 8:28 (NAS): 28 And we know that God causes all things to work together for good to those who love God, to those who are called according to His purpose.

If this is just a bumper sticker slogan, then it's of little comfort in the darkest moments of our lives. However, if this is true, then it becomes our lifeline and our weapon in those same moments to fiercely battle the enemy as we lay claim to this promise and undo his evil scheme to take us out.

The pain of trials and having your character flaws revealed and "surgically" removed is painful. You'd think God would make it easier, but He doesn't. He's not like us. He carries no unhealthy codependency, so our pain doesn't threaten Him. So while He does express sorrow and genuine empathy over the pain of His people, it doesn't make Him uncomfortable to the point of insecurity. Let's be honest, a lot of our own motivation for solving problems for our kids is more about alleviating tension within us and less about what's best for them. Perhaps you've heard the term "helicopter parent" to describe a parent that hovers over their children, ready to intervene at the first whimper or sign of distress - no matter how small. They can't handle the idea of their child enduring difficulty without helping them. On the surface, this may appear loving and healthy, however, it's actually a sign of intense fear deeply rooted in the parent. It's not what is best for the child. Sometimes our children need to fall, skin their knee, and learn. The same is true for us and, of course, when we experience pain, we need comfort from our loving Father, who has promised that He will never leave us. The Holy Spirit lives inside us as our constant companion, ready to administer the grace and peace to get through even the most difficult situations.

JUST LIKE A PHYSICAL WORKOUT REVEALS OUR PHYSICAL LIMITS; TRIALS REVEAL OUR SPIRITUAL CHARACTER AND STRENGTHEN US SO THAT WE CAN CARRY THE HEAVY MANTLE OF AUTHORITY GOD WANTS TO PUT ON US AS HIS KINGS.

Simply put, prevention of difficult circumstances is not the highest goal for us, as parents, nor is it God's highest good for us. He is our comforter, but He's also well aware of the valuable work that takes place in and through suffering and He's not always quick to "make it all better". Just ask Joseph, Paul, Job, David, Daniel, Shadrach, Mishach, and Abednigo, Stephen, the disciples, the apostles, and Jesus! God is not a helicopter parent. He's a parent that walks alongside us. He is the empowering presence and strength His sons draw from to stand under the weight of life's darkest moments. He is the only way Stephen can offer grace while being stoned. He is the only way Paul can go back into a town to preach the love of God after he's been beaten and stoned. He is the only way Shadrach, Mishach, and Abednigo have courage to stand up to the king and endure the fire. Because of His amazing presence with them in the trial, they not only survive the fire, they come out without even smelling like smoke.

Sounds good in theory, but it's actually a hard lesson to learn. Don't lose heart in trials, my brothers. There were - and still are - plenty of miracles, signs and wonders waiting for us in our trials that will prove our Father's nearness and manifest His power to rescue. Again, just ask Joseph, Paul, Job, David, Daniel, Shadrach, Mishach, and Abednigo, Stephen, the disciples, the apostles, and Jesus. Miraculous power is ALWAYS on the agenda for our Father, who loves to show up and show off for His sons.

I can hear the theological gears grinding for those who believe that in God's sovereignty, He orchestrates trials and knows the outcome before we pray. For those who hold this view, it makes no sense to pray for Him to deliver us from a trial. After all, He already knows the outcome, and may have even caused it.

I'd like to suggest that kings must learn to discern the difference between purposeful trials that God uses to make us grow vs. attacks from the enemy that we are supposed to face down and defeat immediately.

These are the deep waters of relationship with Holy Spirit that kings learn to navigate. There is no formulaic answer, but I'll quote one of my mentors who routinely reminds me that Jesus is perfect theology and doctrine. There is no record in scripture of Jesus causing anyone to become sick in order to punish them or teach them a lesson - not even the Pharisees who He openly condemned time and time again. Furthermore, His commands to His followers were to do the same things (miracles), and even greater things than He did. Jesus clearly ascribes evil works to the devil, and deliverance FROM evil works to His Heavenly Father when He explains in simple terms to the Pharisees in Matthew 12:22-30 that a kingdom divided against itself cannot stand. I.e., God isn't causing pain and evil, He's eradicating it. Seems clear enough to me.

KINGS MUST LEARN TO DISCERN THE DIFFERENCE BETWEEN PURPOSEFUL TRIALS THAT GOD USES TO MAKE US GROW VS. ATTACKS FROM THE ENEMY THAT WE ARE SUPPOSED TO FACE DOWN AND DEFEAT IMMEDIATELY.

However, there are teaching moments like the one recorded in Matthew 14:22 where He sends them out into a boat only to get caught up in a ferocious wind storm. Training moment or enemy attack? Both? Whatever it was, it is the moment where Jesus walks out to them on the water in a terrifying display of power and Simon Peter literally gets to follow in Jesus' footsteps.

Ultimately, I'm less concerned with the why/how of trials and more concerned with how we show up as kings and the fruit that trials produce when we're aligned with the truth of Heaven and walking in the power of the Holy Spirit.

Alignment enables us to manifest the Kingdom on Earth and destroy the works of the Devil as Jesus did. I'd suggest that kings have a commission from Jesus in Matthew 10:8 to heal the sick, raise the dead, cleanse the lepers, and cast out demons. We believe Jesus' words in John 14:12 when He declares that we will do greater works than He did. We agree with Jesus in Mark 16:17 when He tells the crowds that signs and wonders will follow those who believe in Him. Kings choose to come under the same mandate Jesus states in Luke 4:18-19, when He quotes Isaiah 61 to declare His purpose for coming to Earth.

> *The Spirit of the Lord is upon me, for he has anointed me to bring Good News to the poor. He has sent me? proclaim that captives will be released, that the blind will see, that the oppressed will be set free, 19 and that the time of the Lord's favor has come."*

We embrace the mantle of authority and the signs, miracles, and wonders seen in the Acts church as our own present day reality. Like our big brother, Jesus, kings understand that humanity is born into the kingdom of Earth where our enemy has overtaken families, cities and nations and put them under His demonic oppression in the unseen realm. Our great commission is to disciple nations and liberate humanity through the revelation of God's superior Kingdom.

So how do God's sons become strong, reliable, loyal, and trustworthy? How do we develop the character that doesn't give into temptation to become proud and arrogant when favor and promotion come? How do we really know if we've put our faith in Him or in our skill sets and abilities to control our circumstances, possessions, or positions? How do we put ourselves into a position to witness firsthand the miraculous signs and wonders of our King? How do we access peace that passes understanding or draw near to Him as our great comforter and friend? Well, again, just ask Joseph, Paul, Job, David, Daniel, Shadrach, Mishach, and Abednigo, Stephen, the disciples, the apostles, and Jesus. Their greatest moments with their Heavenly Father came from some of their darkest trials. Nothing "tees up" the love, grace, and power of the Holy Spirit like a trial. These are the moments in our life when Pharaoh's army is chasing us from behind and in front of us lies a sea that we can't cross. This is the moment when kings tune their hearts to hear the voice of their Father say, "My precious son, do not fear, be still, remain in me, see your victory unfold." Our lofty theories about God get forged into practical realities in the fire of trials. So, kings, my only question for you is this. Do you value the fire?

> *James 1:2-7 (Phillips translation): 8 When all kinds of trials and temptations crowd into your lives my brothers, **don't resent them** as intruders, but welcome them as friends! Realise that they come to test your faith and to produce in you the quality of endurance. But let the process go on until that endurance is fully developed, and you will find you have become men of mature character with the right sort of independence.*

For a king, the answer is "Yes". There is a place reserved for kings in the Kingdom where we can face trials, challenges, and giants with supernatural, unshakable confidence. Not only are we learning to be unafraid, but can be filled with hope because we know the outcome. We fight from victory, not towards it. In this context, James tells us we can welcome trials as friends. As we learned in previous chapters, our reality in Christ positions us in a different Kingdom where different rules apply. We already know what's on the other side of our challenges, just like Jesus, who, for the joy set before him, endured the cross.

> *Hebrews 12:1–2 (NLT): Therefore, since we are surrounded by such a huge crowd of witnesses to the life of faith, let us strip off every weight that slows us down, especially the sin that so easily trips us up. And let us run with endurance the race God has set before us. 2 We do this by keeping our eyes on Jesus, the champion who initiates and perfects our faith. Because of the joy awaiting him, he endured the cross, disregarding its shame. Now he is seated in the place of honor beside God's throne.*

Payday is coming, healing is coming, restoration and victory ARE coming. We may not always get our prayers answered with the breakthrough we expected or even wanted, but breakthrough is ALWAYS coming - that's how life in the Kingdom works. Even as we say goodbye to loved ones, we stand victorious over death and the grave through Christ. Even as we face failure in business, marriage, or ministry, we receive the promises that His grace is sufficient for us and His power is made perfect in our weakness. Regardless of the pain, the trauma, the challenge, we can claim the promise of Romans 8:28 that reminds us all things work together for our good, for those who are called according to His purpose. Kings, that means YOU.

In difficult seasons, we cling to these promises and maintain hope - even in the pain - and we wait because we know our victory and promotion is waiting for us. This has helped me reframe my own mindset. I don't do this perfectly, but on my best days I see my trials as an opportunity to lean deeper into my relationship with Holy Spirit, receive His comfort, learn about myself, and discover how to defeat my enemy. Kings, instead of wasting our lives attempting to avoid and insulate ourselves from hardships, it is our right and privilege to adopt a Kingdom mindset and recognize that we are on assignment to love and heal a broken world.

The Bible says we move from "glory to glory". We'd all like to embrace an oversimplified view of this promise where trials are not part of the process, but instead we can simply "bind and loose" our way out of any situation we don't like. The James passage above suggests that patient endurance is actually the path to maturity.

In my family, we've adopted a practical approach to face trials, honestly taking our cues from King David.

STEP ONE - GET REAL.

I tell my children that your first reaction is a "freebie". When life hits you with a challenge, your knee jerk reaction can be frustration, fear, panic, whatever. Go ahead. Have this moment. Don't clamp down on the emotions, instead give them a voice and express them honestly. Rant, complain, cry, let God have it. He can take it. I'd like to suggest that one of the most precious qualities kings possess is authenticity. Whether in trial or triumph, David models this authenticity in the Psalms as he provides us a behind-the-scenes peek at his highest highs and darkest lows. See his beautiful and honest lament below.

> *Psalm Psalm 31:9–17 (NAS): Be gracious to me, O Lord, for I am in distress;*
>
> *My eye is wasted away from grief, my soul and my body also.*
>
> *10 For my life is spent with sorrow*
>
> *And my years with sighing;*
>
> *My strength has failed because of my iniquity,*
>
> *And my body has wasted away.*
>
> *11 Because of all my adversaries, I have become a reproach,*
>
> *Especially to my neighbors,*
>
> *And an object of dread to my acquaintances;*
>
> *Those who see me in the street flee from me.*
>
> *12 I am forgotten as a dead man, out of mind;*
>
> *I am like a broken vessel.*
>
> *13 For I have heard the slander of many,*
>
> *Terror is on every side;*
>
> *While they took counsel together against me,*
>
> *They schemed to take away my life.*
>
> *14 But as for me, I trust in You, O Lord,*
>
> *I say, "You are my God."*
>
> *15 My times are in Your hand;*
>
> *Deliver me from the hand of my enemies and from those who persecute me.*

> *16 Make Your face to shine upon Your servant;*
> *Save me in Your lovingkindness.*
> *17 Let me not be put to shame, O Lord, for I call upon You;*
> *Let the wicked be put to shame, let them be silent in Sheol.*

This kind of honesty is valuable to God. I've met so many emotionally closed off men who are "fine" all the time. Reality is that when we're pretending everything is fine, we're not hiding our real, raw emotions or pain from God, we're just disconnected out of self-protection. We might be fooling others, but our Heavenly Father is not so easily duped. And in His mercy, He will poke holes in our defenses in order to cultivate a REAL relationship with us because He knows we can't be fully loved until we're fully known. Our King isn't handing out the mantle of His great power and authority to sons that He doesn't fully know, or sons who don't know themselves.

Kings value the truth. Authenticity, by definition, is the truth. Any disconnection from internal authenticity and we can travel down a dangerous path of double-mindedness where we say one thing, but think another. Our enemy will help us justify this disconnect based on the audience, or the circumstances, and will try to convince us we're doing the right thing. We're not. We're allowing the author of lies to influence our minds and mouths. If left unchecked for long enough, we can drift to the point where we can hardly believe what we're saying, or worse, what we're doing.

A religious spirit tempts us to put on a happy face and keep it together on the outside, regardless of whatever pain we're experiencing on the inside. How many of us have fallen into this subtle trap to project an outward appearance of peace or spiritual "maturity" while our inner world is in turmoil? Keeping up external appearances by reciting "Sunday School" answers isn't real maturity, it's a facade. You get no credit for putting on a brave face while pain, shame, and weakness grow and fester on the inside. God loves us too much to allow us to live a lie and the ministry, family, children, or job that appears so perfect from the outside will eventually collapse if the foundation is weakened by inauthenticity or false spirituality perpetuated by a religious spirit.

The spirit of religion Jesus confronted during His ministry is still attacking the Church today. It masquerades as true spirituality, but Jesus recognized it for what it was and called it out in Matthew 23 when he said:

> *Matthew 23:27–28 (NAS): Woe to you, scribes and Pharisees, hypocrites! For you are like whitewashed tombs which on the outside appear beautiful, but inside they are full of dead men's bones and all uncleanness. 28 "So you, too, outwardly appear righteous to men, but inwardly you are full of hypocrisy and lawlessness.*

When kings are aligned with the spirit of religion, they create an unhealthy performance-based culture of shame that only cares about the external appearances and behavior, and neglects the inner world where people are enslaved to sin that is killing them. This inner mess is always revealed eventually, especially during times of stress.

He won't rest His glory on a pretentious prince that is self-deceived about his abilities, strengths, or weaknesses. He wants humble kings, who know where their source of power comes from and who are self-aware. Lamentation is one of the most sincere forms of worship - because it's real. So don't pretend. Get real. Be your authentic self in the valley of the shadow of death. Make noise, let it be messy, rant and rave, whine and complain, let God see the real you and, most importantly, let YOURSELF see the real you. The happy clappy worship offered to God from a disengaged or disappointed heart isn't helping you and lies don't move God's heart. Don't forget, He wants your heart - your real heart - not the counterfeit smile you bring to church. Real kings are good at being real.

STEP TWO - TAKE INVENTORY

The next thing we do in our family is take a practical inventory of the situation. Losing income has practical implications and is cause for alarm. The betrayal from the friend or family member that breaks our trust and hurts us deeply. Don't sugarcoat the trauma, the pain, and the reality of your trial. Consider how the situation affects you emotionally and practically.

STEP THREE - WHAT IS THE TRUTH

The next thing we do in our family is arrest the lies the enemy is speaking into that situation. Kings, this is hard to do, but it's necessary. It may require listening to others around you for perspective, and that's not easy. Again I look to King David for guidance in this situation as I read the story of his crushing defeat at the hand of the Amalekites in 1 Samuel 30.

THE HAPPY CLAPPY WORSHIP OFFERED TO GOD FROM A DISENGAGED OR DISAPPOINTED HEART ISN'T HELPING YOU AND LIES DON'T MOVE GOD'S HEART. REAL KINGS ARE GOOD AT BEING REAL.

1 Samuel 30:1–20 (NLT): Three days later, when David and his men arrived home at their town of Ziklag, they found that the Amalekites had made a raid into the Negev and Ziklag; they had crushed Ziklag and burned it to the ground. 2 They had carried off the women and children and everyone else but without killing anyone.

3 When David and his men saw the ruins and realized what had happened to their families, 4 they wept until they could weep no more. 5 David's two wives, Ahinoam from Jezreel and Abigail, the widow of Nabal from Carmel, were among those captured. 6 David was now in great danger because all his men were very bitter about losing their sons and daughters, and they began to talk of stoning him. But David found strength in the Lord his God.

7 Then he said to Abiathar the priest, "Bring me the ephod!" So Abiathar brought it. 8 Then David asked the Lord, "Should I chase after this band of raiders? Will I catch them?"

And the Lord told him, "Yes, go after them. You will surely recover everything that was taken from you!"

9 So David and his 600 men set out, and they came to the brook Besor. 10 But 200 of the men were too exhausted to cross the brook, so David continued the pursuit with 400 men.

11 Along the way they found an Egyptian man in a field and brought him to David. They gave him some bread to eat and water to drink. 12 They also gave him part of a fig cake and two clusters of raisins, for he hadn't had anything to eat or drink for three days and nights. Before long, his strength returned.

13 "To whom do you belong, and where do you come from?" David asked him.

"I am an Egyptian—the slave of an Amalekite," he replied. "My master abandoned me three days ago because I was sick. 14 We were on our way back from raiding the Kerethites in the Negev, the territory of Judah, and the land of Caleb, and we had just burned Ziklag."

15 "Will you lead me to this band of raiders?" David asked.

The young man replied, "If you take an oath in God's name that you will not kill me or give me back to my master, then I will guide you to them."

16 So he led David to them, and they found the Amalekites spread out across the fields, eating and drinking and dancing with joy because of the vast amount of plunder they had taken from the Philistines and the land of Judah. 17 David and his men rushed in among them and slaughtered them throughout that night and the entire next day until evening. None of the Amalekites escaped except 400 young men who fled on camels. 18 David got back everything the Amalekites had taken, and he rescued his two

> *wives. 19 Nothing was missing: small or great, son or daughter, nor anything else that had been taken. David brought everything back. 20 He also recovered all the flocks and herds, and his men drove them ahead of the other livestock. "This plunder belongs to David!" they said.*

He could have given into the lies that the devil was undoubtedly bombarding him with, "... you're a failure.... you can't even protect your own family.... you're a horrible leader... you've hurt your own men and their families.... you're completely disqualified from being king... God has abandoned you..."

Instead, in the face of a devastating personal loss, David humbly, desperately, seeks God. He strengthened himself as he heard his Father's voice reassure him he would recover all that was taken from him. He received the strategy for redemption, renewed his hope in the Lord, and came out victorious.

In my own life, I've experienced loss and been the victim of various schemes and attacks. In these moments, my enemy invites me to a pity party where I'm the guest of honor and he reminds me I am a victim. It's easy to attend this party because, based on the circumstantial evidence, it's true. However, is there a higher truth? What is Holy Spirit saying and what does the word of God say? The word of God tells me I am more than a conqueror, not a victim. If I partner with my enemy and take on the victim identity, then bitterness and anger will trap me. Been there, done that, and I never want to go back to that sorrowful and hopeless prison.

Let me spend some time here because this is vitally important. Kings, we must not hate on our past, present, or future challenges. Inheritance is reserved for those who overcome. There are so many scriptures about enduring that it's difficult to narrow it down to just one. So I didn't.

James 1:12 (NAS): 12 <u>Blessed is a man who perseveres under trial;</u> for once he has been approved, he will receive the crown of life which the Lord has promised to those who love Him.

Matthew 10:22–23 (NAS): 22 "You will be hated by all because of My name, <u>but it is the one who has endured to the end who will be saved</u> 23 "But whenever they persecute you in one city, flee to the next; for truly I say to you, you will not finish going through the cities of Israel until the Son of Man comes.

Matthew 24:11–14 (NAS): 11 "Many false prophets will arise and will mislead many. 12 "Because lawlessness is increased, most people's love will grow cold. 13 "<u>But the one who endures to the end, he will be saved</u>. 14 "This gospel of the kingdom shall be preached in the whole world as a testimony to all the nations, and then the end will come.

Mark 13:12–13 (NAS): 12 "Brother will betray brother to death, and a father his child; and children will rise up against parents and have them put to death.

13 "You will be hated by all because of My name, <u>but the one who endures to the end, he will be saved.</u>

1 Corinthians 13:3–7 (NAS): 3 And if I give all my possessions to feed the poor, and if I surrender my body to be burned, but do not have love, it profits me nothing. 4 Love is patient, love is kind and is not jealous; love does not brag and is not arrogant, 5 does not act unbecomingly; it does not seek its own, is not provoked, does not take into account a wrong suffered, 6 does not rejoice in unrighteousness, but rejoices with the truth; 7 <u>bears all things, believes all things, hopes all things, endures all things.</u>

2 Thessalonians 1:3–4 (NAS): 3 We ought always to give thanks to God for you, brethren, as is only fitting, because your faith is greatly enlarged, and the love of each one of you toward one another grows ever greater; 4 therefore, we ourselves speak proudly of you among the churches of God for your perseverance and faith in the midst of all your persecutions and afflictions which you endure.

2 Timothy 2:2–10 (NAS): 2 The things which you have heard from me in the presence of many witnesses, entrust these to faithful men who will be able to teach others also. 3 Suffer hardship with me, as a good soldier of Christ Jesus. 4 No soldier in active service entangles himself in the affairs of everyday life, so that he may please the one who enlisted him as a soldier. 5 Also if anyone competes as an athlete, he does not win the prize unless he competes according to the rules. 6 The hard-working farmer ought to be the first to receive his share of the crops. 7 Consider what I say, for the Lord will give you understanding in everything. 8 Remember Jesus Christ, risen from the dead, descendant of David, according to my gospel, 9 for which I suffer hardship even to imprisonment as a criminal; but the word of God is not imprisoned. 10 For this reason I endure all things for the sake of those who are chosen, so that they also may obtain the salvation which is in Christ Jesus and with it eternal glory.

2 Timothy 4:5–8 (NAS): 5 But you, be sober in all things, endure hardship, do the work of an evangelist, fulfill your ministry. 6 For I am already being poured out as a drink offering, and the time of my departure has come. 7 I have fought the good fight, I have finished the course, I have kept the faith; 8 in the future there is laid up for me the crown of righteousness, which the Lord, the righteous Judge, will award to me on that day; and not only to me, but also to all who have loved His appearing.

James 5:10–11 (NAS): 10 As an example, brethren, of suffering and patience, take the prophets who spoke in the name of the Lord. 11 We count those blessed who endured. You have heard of the endurance of Job and have seen the outcome of the Lord's dealings, that the Lord is full of compassion and is merciful.

> *1 Peter 2:18–20 (NAS): 18 Servants, be submissive to your masters with all respect, not only to those who are good and gentle, but also to those who are unreasonable. 19 For this finds favor, if for the sake of conscience toward God a person bears up under sorrows when suffering unjustly. 20 For what credit is there if, when you sin and are harshly treated, you endure it with patience? But if when you do what is right and suffer for it you patiently endure it, this finds favor with God.*

> *2 Timothy 3:12 (NAS): Indeed, all who desire to live godly in Christ Jesus will be persecuted.*

Kings, at whatever point we believed the lie that life is, or should be, a pleasure cruise, we started negotiating our Kingdom destiny. Life is a battleship, you were born into a war, and glorious victory awaits you if you step into your Kingdom destiny. Glorious victory does not mean an easy life, it means a meaningful life of victory over your circumstances, trials, and giants. Victims need not apply. There is no room for victims in the Kingdom. It's fundamentally not who we are anymore. We're dead to sin, alive to Christ, free from the tyrannical rule of our enemy, and walking with Holy Spirit. We have every divine advantage and resource we need to live above our circumstances and walk in victory. If that's not true, then the gospel is a lie and we're all wasting our time. Let that sink in for a minute.

I'm not saying we can't lament. On the contrary, it's actually incredibly healthy to "let God have it" and, as I've said before, He can take it. It's right and authentic to tell Him about your pain and anguish. Don't hold back. The pain needs to come out. As we express it, we must be cautious not to allow ourselves to align our mindsets with the demon named "Victim" in the process. If we do, he'll ruin our life by framing up ALL our experiences through his lenses of victimhood. There's a big difference between expressing authentic grief in the wake of tragedy and loss and allowing this evil spirit to take up semi-permanent residence in your life. You'll know if he's hanging around because you'll gradually shift away from a hopeful mindset into a pessimistic attitude that expects the worst to happen. This mindset believes God has abandoned you and people are out to hurt you. Victim ALWAYS is frustrated whenever it faces a new trial. Real kings have discovered that we're not obligated to be RE-freak-out every time we face a new trial. We can face challenges, tragedies, and trials with peace, confidence, even a measure of joy. This challenge to express honest pain and yet maintain hope is so real. We see it as we read how Job laments his situation, but simultaneously praises God and acknowledges His power, supremacy, and goodness. This is definitely deep water. Kings, if we don't learn this, I'd suggest we'll not be able to lead ourselves into abundant life, much less our families, cities, churches, businesses, or nations.

Allowing this victim mindset to take root grieves the Holy Spirit, disconnects us from Heavenly resources of power and hope, stifles our growth, and sidelines us from walking in our full identity and authority. Our trials and struggles are liberating us from dysfunction, fear, doubt, and weakness. This is the plan and the process. If we get it, we'll get our inheritance and become trustworthy kings. If we don't, we'll wander in the desert, whine, complain, die, and our kids will inherit the Promised Land. Think I'm wrong? Recall the story of the Israelites who wandered in the desert for 40 years after they were liberated from Egypt because they made excuses for why they couldn't obey God. They saw the giants in their promised land and shrank back, whined, complained, and took on the identity of victims instead of God's chosen people upon whom His favor and blessing rested. Because of this, God took care of them like a loving Father for 40 years in the desert by miraculously providing food, water, and guidance day and night. But He never let them inherit the Promised Land until an entire generation of "victims" had died, and the next generation of overcomers and giant killers was ready to go to war and possess the land under Joshua's leadership. This generation saw God do amazing things to route their enemies before their very eyes and followed God with courage.

God loves you and doesn't want you to be a victim. Your lions and bears prepare you for your Goliaths. Never forget, it's the little stones that fell giants. The world would use a machine gun, God uses a boy, a man, after his heart, and a slingshot. The comparison between David and Saul will hopefully illustrate the difference between a victim king and a overcoming, warrior king.

When the battle heats up, Davids get their heart right before God. As we see time and time again in the Psalms, David would go into his secret place, worship, pray, connect with God's heart, and then come out and conquer his enemy in the power of the Spirit.

Sauls take inventory of their skills, army, population, network, associates, alliances, likes, status, friends, family, last name, platform... you get the idea. This process creates its own torment because "Sauls" recognize that systems of men are merely forms with no real power and they may not be enough to win the battle they face. The Holy Spirit, on the other hand, is raw power and "Davids" perceive it. As one of my mentors and spiritual fathers likes to say, "One person, walking with God, is always in the majority."

Jesus himself models this strategy in the same ways. He didn't use systems of men to show His power. He didn't overthrow Roman authority or occupation. He didn't even attempt to provoke a coup within the Jewish community. He simply connected with his Father, regularly, privately, and then did what the Father said to do, and said what the Father told him to say. In so doing, He asserted supreme authority over the unseen second realm, which gave Him authority over the first realm. In short, that was how He inherited the power to set captives free. The King and his Kingdom are not a form - powerless ideas or philosophies without impact. The King of Kings has all authority to speak and move any mountain, take any territory, and conquer any giant. You're adopted into that family, and legal heir to that relationship, process, authority and power. Kings in the Kingdom do not gain power or position through the same means you see modeled by the lesser kings of the Earth. Instead, they listen to their Heavenly Father, the King of Kings, and do what He says. As a result, they move in real, raw, uncontested power to glorify their King, just like their big brother, Jesus, did.

STEP FOUR - CELEBRATE

In my family, we added this step because we're always looking for a reason to party (several of us are Enneagram 7s). And what better reason to celebrate than to be a living example of how God works all things together for good? I believe that one of the most important parts of this process is to commemorate and celebrate our testimonies of God's deliverance, and faithfulness even when we're still in the process of gaining our promotion and victory over our enemy. In our house we've even had celebratory meals in the middle of battles, because as Psalm 23 says:

> *Psalm 23:5 (NLT): You prepare a feast for me*
>
> *in the presence of my enemies.*

What better way to remind the devil of his ultimate failure than having a celebratory meal in his presence before the victory has been manifested? I love that this is the confidence we can have in our position as kings of a superior Kingdom under the reign and rule of our totally trustworthy and loving King of Kings.

So, to recap, kings:

1. Are good at being real with the emotions of painful events, trials, and trauma
2. Can inventory the situation and understand the real implications and impact.

3. Are good at detecting and arresting the lies of the enemy and are superb at seeking the Holy Spirit to speak truth, wisdom, and strategy for their deliverance and miraculous breakthrough
4. Celebrate their breakthrough and victories, as well as the triumphs of those around them

Kings, when we get good at this process, we change the culture around us. No longer do we, nor the people we lead, view problems or trials as reasons to panic. Instead, we can mine the gold from every unique circumstance, whether good or bad.

King's, you know what to do. Let's realign our mindsets with Heaven, face our trials with our King of Kings, and let them do their work. Just like the 4th man shows up in the fire with Shadrach, Mishak, and Abednigo, you'll be amazed at how your King shows up in your "furnace" moments and forges a bond of trust with you that will empower you for your assignment. Your faith will be stronger, your love and loyalty to your King deeper, and you probably won't even smell like smoke.

Chapter 9

CHINKS IN THE ARMOR
INSECURITY

17 As the Scriptures say, "If you want to boast, boast only about the Lord." 18 When people commend themselves, it doesn't count for much. The important thing is for the Lord to commend them.

—2 CORINTHIANS 10:17–18 (NLT)

I hesitated to even write about this topic because it seems so elementary to be talking to kings about this, and yet, I regularly am astonished at the levels of insecurity I see in leaders in nearly every sphere of my life. As I read about how the disciples argued over who was greatest in the Kingdom, I realize that I'm not so different. When I struggle with insecurity and the pursuit of significance, I'm in good company. To start, I suggest we look at insecurity at a very basic level and understand it as symptomatic of a greater disease called Identity Crisis. And I'd also like to identify some of the awkward learned behaviors I've observed in kings who've grown up in environments filled with insecurity. Social graces and fruits of the Spirit like peace, patience, kindness, are to flow from the mouths and actions of kings. But if we're socially unaware or untrained in these graces because of poor examples of kingship in our lives, they can be a blind spot.

I also think this is a relevant topic for kings because we live in a world today where insecurity is at an all-time high for everyone. People are insecure about jobs, money, relationships, the future, the past, the present, social situations, conflict, pandemics, politics, wars, you name it. Kings are not immune to this and as we have learned, the devil actively speaks lies into the situations and circumstances of our life that steal, kill, and destroy our confidence and our identity. The pace of life is so fast that if I'm not careful, I can easily bounce from one situation to the next, hardly aware of his influence.

Whether it's putting our best face forward in an interaction with a superior at work, or navigating a relationship with a loved one, it's remarkable how much of our energy is spent "hiding" behind some level of insecurity, seeking affirmation, attempting to avoid rejection, trying to shift blame, trying to gain favor, etc.

One specific way we attempt to navigate this dilemma is to manipulate people's perceptions of us by boasting. Within the first few minutes of any interaction, you can typically identify the telltale signs of insecurity if you know what to listen for.

If a person...

- figures out how to shift the conversation to talk about themselves, vs. continuing to take an interest in the other person...
- finds a way to name-drop in the first few minutes of the conversation...
- talks about their public or professional accomplishments as a way of identifying themselves...

You get the idea.

We all know people like this and to be honest, they can be annoying to be around. But honestly, haven't we all struggled with insecurity and given in to the temptation to boast and brag in order to hide our insecurity from those around us? I certainly have.

Deep down, I think most of us know the answer is not boasting about ourselves, who we know, or what we've done. That's the trap the enemy sets to get us to project a false persona and to attach our worth to the affirmation of our peers. In Proverbs, Solomon shares some very practical and important wisdom for this dilemma.

> *Proverbs 29:25 (NAS): The fear of man brings a snare, But he who trusts in the Lord will be exalted.*

Sadly, the affirmation of your peers is fleeting, performance-based, and will never satisfy. Instead, is a trap that trips and captures you. Let's face it, there will always be someone more accomplished, talented, charismatic, and who knows "bigger" people than we do. Real kings don't waste time in the elusive pursuit of value through the affirmation of people. Favor with men is a gift from God for faithful obedience. If we can't resolve this, we will never be good kings. We will run from relational conflict, avoid hard decisions, and allow our true convictions to be bullied by stronger personalities or peer pressure in our environment.

REAL KINGS DON'T WASTE TIME IN THE ELUSIVE PURSUIT OF VALUE THROUGH THE AFFIRMATION OF PEOPLE. FAVOR WITH MEN IS A GIFT FROM GOD FOR FAITHFUL OBEDIENCE. IF WE CAN'T RESOLVE THIS, WE WILL NEVER BE GOOD KINGS.

If you're a believer in Jesus Christ, you have a unique advantage in overcoming insecurity. Hebrews 12:2 tells us that Jesus endured the cross for the joy set before him and in John 3:16, we learn that God so loved the world that He gave his son to die as a sin offering in our place. This means that as He was hanging on the cross in pain,

He was filled with joy as he thought about YOU. He was so overjoyed to set YOU free it strengthened Him to endure the pain and shame of the cross. I'd suggest that if we could wrap our minds around the reality that the all-powerful creator of the universe holds us in such high esteem then we'd find it EASY to gain victory over the temptation to seek the praise of man, pander to the crowds, or live with any level of insecurity.

The cross was the most important commendation you could ever receive... better than a promotion, or accolades from peers or colleagues. It's better than receiving an award for doing something amazing or expanding your social media following.

Jesus himself warns His disciples about boasting that demons listen to them and obey. In Luke 10:20, He instructs them not to boast that demons listen to them, but instead to be glad that their names are registered in Heaven. Translation: God knows your name. That's enough. Don't be over impressed with your supernatural gifts or get a big head about the fact that you can control demons.

One of my favorite examples of true security and self-confidence is John the Baptist. John the Baptist was a pretty "big deal" in his day, especially after he baptized Jesus, his cousin and the Messiah, the Son of God. But he did not feel the need to assert himself to establish his value, and it made him an incredible man, a wise teacher, and a trustworthy king. Think about it. He carried kingdom revelation to such a great degree that he started a *baptism* ministry of repentance in a culture that had NO grid for it. Remember that under Mosaic law, Jews at this time would have understood animal sacrifice as the normal method for atonement of sins - not baptism. It's possible that's why we see a debate break out with a Jewish leader about "ceremonial cleansing" in the John passage below. Regardless, we see that Jesus followed suit and began baptizing people in the same way after He was baptized by John. John's disciples were insecure about this new guy stealing their thunder and brought it to John's attention in frustration. John handles it with grace as a secure and confident king.

John 3:22–36 (NLT): 22 Then Jesus and his disciples left Jerusalem and went into the Judean countryside. Jesus spent some time with them there, baptizing people.

23 At this time John the Baptist was baptizing at Aenon, near Salim, because there was plenty of water there; and people kept coming to him for baptism. 24 (This was before John was thrown into prison.) 25 A debate broke out between John's disciples and a certain Jew over ceremonial cleansing.26 So John's disciples came to him and said, "Rabbi, the man you met on the other side of the Jordan River, the one you identified as the Messiah, is also baptizing people. And everybody is going to him instead of coming to us."

27 John replied, "No one can receive anything unless God gives it from heaven. 28 You yourselves know how plainly I told you, 'I am not the Messiah. I am only here to prepare the way for him.' 29 It is the bridegroom who marries the bride, and the bridegroom's friend is simply glad to stand with him and hear his vows. Therefore, I am filled with joy at his success. 30 He must become greater and greater, and I must become less and less.

31 "He has come from above and is greater than anyone else. We are of the earth, and we speak of earthly things, but he has come from heaven and is greater than anyone else. 32 He testifies about what he has seen and heard, but how few believe what he tells them! 33 Anyone who accepts his testimony can affirm that God is true. 34 For he is sent by God. He speaks God's words, for God gives him the Spirit without limit. 35 The Father loves his Son and has put everything into his hands. 36 And anyone who believes in God's Son has eternal life. Anyone who doesn't obey the Son will never experience eternal life but remains under God's angry judgment."

John the Baptist had gained a following, had disciples, and his influence and ministry were growing. How many of us in that situation would begin dreaming about the future and where this ministry could go?

Or how many would be deflated to hear about another person having success in promoting *our* message? We may be kings, but an insecure orphan spirit can still attack if/when we let our guard down.

John didn't seem to have these insecurities. What a beautiful heart. John's disciples get frustrated at the fact that Jesus is baptizing people because they believe that's THEIR thing. If I were speaking at a conference and right before I went out to give my talk, the speaker right before me gave the same message, I wonder how I would respond. I wonder how my team would respond.

John quickly rebukes his disciples and gets their minds back in alignment with reality. He reminds them he has never claimed to be the Messiah, and he spells out the reality of who Jesus is, His gifts and purpose, and how Jesus is literally the greatest human that's ever lived.

Then John shares the knockout punch to insecurity. He doesn't just tell his disciples to tolerate the situation. He shares his incredible joy at Jesus' success and promotes Jesus above himself, declaring that Jesus must increase and he must decrease. They must have got the message because later we see that some of John's disciples become Jesus' disciples.

Rubber meets road time. When another king gets recognized over you, do you celebrate? Do you have joy at the success of another king, even if it comes at the expense of your ministry, business, reputation? Do you actively seek to promote another person when you see the favor of God's on them?

Kings of the Earth are horrible at this, and sadly, many kings in the Kingdom of Heaven are as well. Jealousy, competition, and an orphan spirit are rampant among God's sons. Guys, we need to lighten up. You have been given all things in Christ and no one can take that away. We need to take a breath and remember David. He sought nothing except to be in close, unbroken fellowship with the God who made the stars that served as his roof in the wilderness. Like John, David had a pure heart.

This is tough stuff, but unfortunately I humbly suggest this is an important gate that stands between you and your next promotion in the Kingdom. God isn't negotiating on matters of the heart. If your heart isn't pure, you'll crumble during the battle. Promoting you to any level of success or influence could be your inevitable downfall and Holy Spirit is too merciful for that. He doesn't want to set us up to fail. We all have grand visions of how we'll show up in battle, trials, tough circumstances. We envision that we'll be strong, stable, selfless, even philanthropic to those around us. We often fancy ourselves as the knight in shining armor, but He knows better.

Reality is that many of us crumble in the heat of battle and this reveals a heart condition that isn't ready for the weight of glory. Psalm 24 poses the question, "Who can ascend the hill of the Lord?" And then quickly answers the question - those with clean hands and a pure heart - people like John the Baptist.

Your gut-check assignment - find a person or business or ministry who may be in "competition" with you and find a success of theirs that you can celebrate. Give them glory, honor, and praise. Find a business, ministry, co-worker or colleague you can honor - even perhaps someone that has wronged you in the past. One caveat, make it genuine. Celebrate a real success, a real accomplishment worthy of praise.

If you do this, and it doesn't grind your gears, then you're probably on your way to purity of heart like John the Baptist - well done. If your internal monologue doesn't match the praise coming out of your mouth, and you sense bitterness, resentment, jealousy, etc, then you've got some work to do. Remember this one thing from the passage above, no one can receive anything unless God gives it from heaven. Take a minute, repent, receive forgiveness, then forgive yourself. Ask for Holy Spirit to help to walk away from self-promotion and to help you grow in your ability to practice other-promotion. Your next promotion is on the other side of this test. Trust me, jealousy and all of his ugly friends will not be allowed to make the trip into your Promised Land. You're bound for glory and an inheritance literally fit for a king. Holy Spirit won't allow those critters to come along for the ride and your objective is not to hide them in your luggage, but to get rid of them. Partner with Holy Spirit, cut them off, and get healed so you can make the journey with your heart intact.

Next time you feel insecurity settle in, or are tempted to assert your own worth by bragging to gain status in the eyes of other people, remember this. There is nothing more significant than the full, unconditional approval of God the Father through the miraculous work of Christ on the cross. You'll never be more loved than that. You've been adopted as a son, co-heir with Jesus, and positioned as royalty in an eternal Kingdom that will last far longer, and carry far more weight and power, than any position or status this Earth can offer.

You can relax. The pressure to perform is officially gone. You've already "arrived" in the most important way imaginable. You've been received and are honored by the most important person ever. The Lord Himself walks with you, He talks to you, He helps you, He loves you, and has given you the gift of eternal significance.

So how does this work itself out in practical ways? Here are some tips in case you have never observed healthy, secure kings interact with those around them.

- Take inventory of your inner world - become familiar with what insecurity feels like and when you feel it coming on, bind it and send it back to hell where it came from. It's a lie and you can and should deal with it ruthlessly. Ask your constant friend and companion, Holy Spirit, to reveal the truth of your identity and value.

- When interacting with others, talk less, listen more. Listen with intentionality and genuine interest.

- Make eye contact and smile - again, these are basic social graces that kings exhibit to show confidence and ease. Kings are keenly aware of how their non-verbal communication impacts people and their environment. As a king, you have been appointed to be an ambassador of reconciliation, as we read in 2 Corinthians 5:18. So think about how you carry yourself as you interact with the world around you. Think about what it literally looks like to walk with a posture of power, grace, humility, kindness, and dignity that fully represents the superior Kingdom of Heaven.

This is by no means an exhaustive list, but allow this to be your starting place as you partner with Holy Spirit to step into a royal identity, put on your kingly robes, and represent the King of Kings. You'll be amazed at how powerful and confident you feel, how well received you are, and how much the King's grace and favor will increase upon you.

Chapter 10

PANIC IS OPTIONAL

Kings are perpetual students. One of our ongoing educational pursuits as a king is self-reflection aimed at identifying specific internal disconnects between what the Bible says about how you are to live and how you really live. This is an ongoing exploration of the gap between who you are when you're at your best and who you are the rest of the time - and why there is a gap in the first place. As we engage in this process, we seek to understand who we are in our current state, who it is that Holy Spirit is making us into, and what barriers, or lies, stand in our way.

For years, I've been attempting to gain wisdom as I reflect on my own gap. As a king, how am I expected to "show up" when problems arise in my personal life? Do I act in a manner worthy of my calling, as Paul instructs in Ephesians 4:1, or do I revert to old habits and selfishness?

As kings, I believe we must be ruthlessly honest about this self-evaluation. Dishonest self-assessment will get us nowhere. Old mindsets and paradigms are just not going to get us to the "abundant" life that we are promised as our inheritance in Christ, so why protect or hide them? Old mindsets make it IMPOSSIBLE to become a king. Romans 8 says so much. Brace yourselves for a scripture avalanche of awesomeness! Feast on it, savor it, and let's unpack some parts of it together.

Romans 8:1–39 (NLT): Chapter 8

So now there is no condemnation for those who belong to Christ Jesus. 2 And because you belong to him, the power of the life-giving Spirit has freed you from the power of sin that leads to death. 3
The law of Moses was unable to save us because of the weakness of our sinful nature. So God did what the law could not do. He sent his own Son in a body like the bodies we sinners have. And in that body God declared an end to sin's control over us by giving his Son as a sacrifice for our sins. 4 He did this so that the just requirement of the law would be fully satisfied for us, who no longer follow our sinful nature but instead follow the Spirit.

5 Those who are dominated by the sinful nature think about sinful things, but those who are controlled by the Holy Spirit think about things that please the Spirit. 6 So letting your sinful nature control your mind leads to death. But letting the Spirit control your mind leads to life and peace. 7 For the sinful nature is always hostile to God. It never did obey God's laws, and it never will. 8 That's why those who are still under the control of their sinful nature can never please God.

9 But you are not controlled by your sinful nature. You are controlled by the Spirit if you have the Spirit of God living in you. (And remember that those who do not have the Spirit of Christ living in them do not belong to him at all.) 10 And Christ lives within you, so even though your body will die because of sin, the Spirit gives you life because you have been made right with God.
11 The Spirit of God, who raised Jesus from the dead, lives in you. And just as God raised Christ Jesus from the dead, he will give life to your mortal bodies by this same Spirit living within you.

12 Therefore, dear brothers and sisters, you have no obligation to do what your sinful nature urges you to do. 13 For if you live by its dictates, you will die. But if through the power of the Spirit you put to death the deeds of your sinful nature, you will live. 14 For all who are led by the Spirit of God are children of God.

15 So you have not received a spirit that makes you fearful slaves. Instead, you received God's Spirit when he adopted you as his own children. Now we call him, "Abba, Father." 16 For his Spirit joins with our spirit to affirm that we are God's children. 17 And since we are his children, we are his heirs. In fact, together with Christ we are heirs of God's glory. But if we are to share his glory, we must also share his suffering. 18 Yet what we suffer now is nothing compared to the glory he will reveal to us later. 19 For all creation is waiting eagerly for that future day when God will reveal who his children really are. 20 Against its will, all creation was subjected to God's curse. But with eager hope, 21 the creation looks forward to the day when it will join God's children in glorious freedom from death and decay. 22 For we know that all creation has been groaning as in the pains of childbirth right up to the present time. 23 And we believers also groan, even though we have the Holy Spirit within us as a foretaste of future glory, for we long for our bodies to be released from sin and suffering. We, too, wait with eager hope for the day when God will give us our full rights as his adopted children, including the new bodies he has promised us. 24 We were given this hope when we were saved. (If we already have something, we don't need to hope for it. 25 But if we look forward to something we don't yet have, we must wait patiently and confidently.)

26 And the Holy Spirit helps us in our weakness. For example, we don't know what God wants us to pray for. But the Holy Spirit prays for us with groanings that cannot be expressed in words. 27 And the Father who knows all hearts knows what the Spirit is saying, for the Spirit pleads for us believers in harmony with God's own will. 28 And we know that God causes everything to work together for the good of those who love God and are called according to his purpose for them. 29 For God knew his people in advance, and he chose them to become like his Son, so that his Son would be the

> *firstborn among many brothers and sisters. 30 And having chosen them, he called them to come to him. And having called them, he gave them right standing with himself. And having given them right standing, he gave them his glory.*
>
> *Nothing Can Separate Us from God's Love*
>
> *31 What shall we say about such wonderful things as these? If God is for us, who can ever be against us? 32 Since he did not spare even his own Son but gave him up for us all, won't he also give us everything else? 33 Who dares accuse us whom God has chosen for his own? No one—for God himself has given us right standing with himself. 34 Who then will condemn us? No one—for Christ Jesus died for us and was raised to life for us, and he is sitting in the place of honor at God's right hand, pleading for us.*
>
> *35 Can anything ever separate us from Christ's love? Does it mean he no longer loves us if we have trouble or calamity, or are persecuted, or hungry, or destitute, or in danger, or threatened with death? 36 (As the Scriptures say, "For your sake we are killed every day; we are being slaughtered like sheep.") 37 No, despite all these things, overwhelming victory is ours through Christ, who loved us.*
>
> *38 And I am convinced that nothing can ever separate us from God's love. Neither death nor life, neither angels nor demons, neither our fears for today nor our worries about tomorrow—not even the powers of hell can separate us from God's love. 39 No power in the sky above or in the earth below—indeed, nothing in all creation will ever be able to separate us from the love of God that is revealed in Christ Jesus our Lord.*

Let me attempt to unpack this with a beginning premise that may explain where I'm headed.

I'm more convinced now than ever that we - born-again believers and non-believers alike - are increasingly relying on control over our circumstances as a PRIMARY means to measure success and gain peace.

I'd suggest that IF the quality of our marriage, career, kids, car collection... or IF the size of our paycheck, retirement account, boat or house... or IF our good looks, social status, "likes", friend-group, or prestige and acceptance among our peers... or IF our education level... or insurance policies, or government policies, or sphere of influence... or any other external things are the PRIMARY sources of our confidence or happiness in life, THEN we are but one catastrophe away from a psychological breakdown. We're one stock market crash, one car crash, one bad doctor report, one mass shooting at a shopping mall or school, one unexpected death, divorce, fire, hurricane, or earthquake, job loss, or pandemic away from watching our life implode.

Have you been paying attention to the ever-increasing anxiety that plagues almost everyone around you? Have noticed your own fear rising in the aftermath of COVID, wars, political scandals, uncertainty in your work or pain in your relationships?

And yet we live in the most prosperous nation in human history, with more money, options, conveniences, and security than any people group on planet Earth. If your household makes more than $50,000 per year, you're in the top 9% wealthiest people on Earth at this moment in history. Of the Earth's 7+ billion human inhabitants, over 6 billion live on less than $32 per day ($11,680 per year) and over 4 billion don't have access to a clean water source inside their dwelling, but instead must haul water from a clean source to their homes to supply their family's needs.

Ironically, the bigger houses, more money, better insurance, better jobs, bigger retirement accounts, better friends, cars, doctors, medications, etc. that are designed to create security and insulate us from pain, have trapped us in an unending, panic-inducing pursuit of more. This is a very elegant trap.

This dichotomy is the product of an earthbound paradigm of scarcity created by our mortal enemy, and the enemy of our King. It's a second realm lie that presents itself as a truth that cunningly sneaks past our Spirit-man's defenses because it seems "true" intellectually. Therefore, sadly, most people, including believers, build their lives around this lie yet never achieve the security and safety it promises.

In a scarcity mindset, everything is in limited supply, therefore I must accumulate things/wealth/power to be secure and gain an advantage over others through more efficient and effective methods of accumulation. Because my perception of the world around me is that everything is in limited supply, my gain must come at the expense of others. I use my time, energy, and resources, in pursuit of things I believe offer safety, security, and significance.

Yet deep down... don't we all live with an uneasy feeling that it's a lie? Worse, don't we also live with the ongoing fear of the inevitable "storm" that is bearing down on us that threatens our things/wealth/power, and the security and identity they supposedly produce.

This fear temporarily ebbs when our life is good. If we get a promotion, or our medical report is positive, or if our spouse is meeting our needs, then we feel pretty good, confident, hopeful about the future. Right?

But the fear quickly rushes back in with the latest stock market crash, or breaking news story about an active shooter at a local college campus or the latest killer virus, or when you get "that" phone call in the middle of the night because something tragic has happened to someone you love, and your life is changed from that moment on.

If we're honest, many of us are still emotionally tossed around by circumstances and we spend most of our time and energy trying to gain control over our world and inoculate ourselves from pain - physical and emotional - past, present, and future.

In this tension, we cultivate coping mechanisms to escape the sobering reality that, despite our best efforts, we actually don't control most of our life, and it freaks us out. We shop, we look at porn and masturbate; we drink too much; we work too much, we gamble, we do drugs, sleep around, or entertain ourselves non-stop, we cope. And our enemy is more than willing to negotiate the terms of our surrender of the promised abundant life in Christ, in exchange for an all-you-can-eat buffet of flimsy, quick-fixes that promise "life", but only lead to death.

No judgment here. I have used more than my share of coping mechanisms and still do sometimes. But I'm discovering that my new life - in Christ - makes it possible to adopt a new mindset - the mindset of a king who is a citizen of Heaven. A mindset that sees the endless supply and opportunities of Heaven as more real than the scarcity and limited resources present on Earth. I'm learning that I can choose to show up differently in this life by His Spirit, working in me. I'm discovering that for supernatural, storm calming kings, panic is optional.

You can tell a lot about a person's mindset by the way they talk. If my speech is pessimistic, or I dwell on the past, or what's wrong with others, or if I'm fearful, anxious, or worried about circumstances, then I might be "flirting" with a scarcity mindset as a lifestyle. Kings speak words filled with hope, life, and the goodness of their homeland, the Kingdom of Heaven.

As a king, under the direct protection, reign, and rule of the King of Kings, who has been given ALL authority in Heaven and on Earth and beneath the Earth, and who has been given the name above all other names, you officially have permission to abandon a scarcity mindset and anchor your life in something immovable, steadfast, and permanent instead of the ever-changing circumstances around you.

Let me be more clear, If you're a believer, but you dwell more on circumstances around you than you do on the supremacy of God and the Kingdom of Heaven, then you've put your faith in the wrong kingdom and your complaining, doubt, and pessimism is a worship offering to the wrong king.

If this is you, there is hope, but you need to immerse yourself in the truth to break the power of lies embedded in your mindset. You must renew your mind in alignment with the Spirit of God working in you, and fight the temptation to see things simply with your natural intellect or you'll never fully receive the abundant life Jesus paid for on the cross, much less become the king you're destined to become in God's kingdom. You choose your focus. Should you choose intellectual observations and circumstances over the King and His Kingdom, then your pain and frustration are self-inflicted. Jesus paid for you to step up and step into your rightful inheritance and identity as a king. He did NOT pay for you to be a pessimist while you fearfully wait for the proverbial shoe to drop. If that's not a sobering thought, then I question if you have a pulse.

IF YOU'RE A BELIEVER, BUT YOU DWELL MORE ON CIRCUMSTANCES AROUND YOU THAN YOU DO ON THE SUPREMACY OF GOD AND THE KINGDOM OF HEAVEN, THEN YOU'VE PUT YOUR FAITH IN THE WRONG KINGDOM AND YOUR COMPLAINING, DOUBT, AND PESSIMISM IS A WORSHIP OFFERING TO THE WRONG KING.

I'm not suggesting that this is easy. No, quite the opposite. This is a challenging and intentional exercise of realigning your mind with the Kingdom of Heaven and with Spirit of God in you. This is an ongoing process of binding and rejecting the old engrained sinful mindsets that we've inherited, and that we see modeled all around us all the time.

Kings know the difference between a conversion experience that takes place in a moment, and the ongoing work to step into destiny and authority as you cultivate intimacy with Holy Spirit. They are different processes. The first is salvational and gets you into the Kingdom forever - Praise the Lord!!!! The second restores you to your rightful place of governing the Earth and qualifies you to become an inner-circle co-laborer with Christ in building His Kingdom, on Earth as it is in Heaven.

Mature kings are discovering that we're not governed by fear of the unknown or the crisis du jour. We're not the sum of our past failures or current shortcomings. Our significance and security is not defined by the money in the bank, or the size of the house, or our job title. We used to be slaves to this Earthly "wisdom" but Jesus died to set us free from that nonsense and place us in Heavenly realms with Him. My life in the Kingdom is completely governed by the new laws of a superior Kingdom. Laws like goodness, mercy, love, abundance, grace, righteousness, wisdom, revelation, and miracles, just to name a few.

Our new life is governed by a permanent power much stronger and reliable than anything on this earth. No external circumstance can overwhelm the power inside us unless we choose to let it. This power is the Holy Spirit of God, who has taken up residence inside our physical bodies as we've learned in previous chapters. This is truly amazing when you think about it. Kings recognize this is the key that unlocks everything in the Kingdom. The Holy Spirit living in us makes it possible to live with authentic peace, confidence, and life to the fullest. As Paul says in our passage today, Holy Spirit gives us capacity to experience hard circumstances, unfairness, abuse and disappointment and get HEALED instead of devolving into just another angry, bitter, victim.

Holy Spirit empowers us to enter others' brokenness and not be overwhelmed. He makes it possible to live a glorious life and therefore you can become a life-giving, selfless presence in someone else's life. This is what it means to be a king.

Before you read this next portion, a disclaimer. I ABSOLUTELY LOVE the Church. I think it is God's best idea to redeem the Earth right behind Jesus's death and resurrection. In its purest form, the Church, this collection of Spirit-filled born-again human beings living as kings and queens ushering in God's rule and reign on Earth, is the most magnificent thing on the planet. If you don't agree, I'd challenge you to consider Jesus' words in John 16:7. He's quite convinced that the Earth will be better off when He leaves and sends the Holy Spirit to produce a multiplied manifestation of God's glory and power among hundreds, thousands, and millions of humans vs. just one "Jesus".

However, the Church has some "warts" and kings know it. They know that being a true king with divine authority is not an exercise in following the traditions and rules of Catholic**ism**, Method**ism**, Presbyterian**ism**, or any other "**ism**".

True kings see the pitfalls of this mindset for what it is - an attack from a religious spirit designed to undermine the unity of the body of Christ. Wise kings have discovered that religion is powerless to fight real spiritual battles and totally impotent to set captives free. This is because "isms" are incapable of producing freedom, healing, joy or any other REAL fruit. "Isms" are, by default, misrepresentations of the King of Kings and the Kingdom of Heaven. The Kingdom is not fractured, nor divided against itself, therefore any "ism" or group that separates itself from another "ism" or group is, by default, NOT representative of the unified Kingdom of God. It represents the kingdom of our enemy. I realize that's a strong statement, but how can it be wrong? Consider this example. If I'm more concerned about the debate over full immersion baptism vs sprinkling, miracles, sacrament, eschatology, or any other doctrinal difference, and I'm willing to allow my zeal over such an issue to drive a relational wedge between me and an entire group of my spiritual family, how can I claim to be aligned with Heaven? Perhaps the issues listed above are not the Hills your tradition is dying on, maybe it's homosexuality, abortion, or conservative vs liberal politics. Whatever the issues are, if they are not salvational, sinful, or explicitly clarified in Scripture, then they shouldn't create division - ever. Moreover, in my opinion, they should barely come up in doctrinal or theological discussions at all. I believe that even entertaining these issues is flirting with a religious spirit, and I want nothing to do with that being. Debates that are not central and salvational to the Christian faith become fodder for division and distractions that can lead even the strong leaders, churches, and entire denominations off into the spiritual weeds. When this occurs, they become irrelevant and impotent to build the Kingdom and manifest the glory of Heaven in the Earth.

Perhaps the "isms" were well intended, but sadly they've devolved into just another method of control... a way of keeping "clean" people separated from "dirty" people as defined by the "ism". What a poor representation of the Gospel of Jesus and the life we can live through the Holy Spirit's power. Sorry world.

But things are changing...

This broken but beautiful Earth is waiting for the true children of God to show up and be the full embodiment of the good news. It is hungry for the real thing, 100%, non-stop, simple good news just like our big brother Jesus modeled, and just like we can model through the power of Holy Spirit, who is 100%, non-stop good news living inside us. I'd suggest that the world will know the real thing when they see it.

Kings have authentically received the good news first for themselves and have the power to give it away to the world around them. They are not just well-behaved, religious "parrots" or rule-keepers, but sons who have been transformed by the renewing of their mind and the Spirit living inside them.

So are you curious where you are on this journey to step into your kingly identity? One simple assessment is to start by listening to the way you speak. If the voice coming out of you is NOT the voice of the Holy Spirit, then consider NOT speaking. Refrain from adding to the noise. The world is drowning in intellectual content that sounds smart but is rooted in the wrong kingdom and is powerless to produce real fruit.

I believe the days of "sifting" are coming when the imposter kings taking part in this chorus of philosophers could get beat naked and run out of the house... sons of Sceva-style... by a demon who isn't impressed with their "M-div" or their latest best-selling book. I'm not being snarky here and I apologize if this sounds cynical or "ranty". I'm just deeply burdened by the possibility that the beautiful Bride of Christ, His Church, is presently infiltrated by a religious spirit and run by insecure imposter kings who are more concerned about their status than setting captives free.

Kings are not peddlers of self-help nonsense and their life and mindset can't be boiled down to a 3-point pep talk. Their entire life is a wake up call to those around them. Their acts of love and power strike a resonant chord in the Earth that vibrates dead things to life. Their words are like the rain on dry ground, growing holy conviction, repentance, faith, authenticity, humility, power, and wisdom. In short, they produce REAL fruit, born from a superior kingdom that shows others the way to everlasting life, just like Jesus did. They are apostolic culture-makers.

THE WORLD IS DROWNING IN INTELLECTUAL CONTENT THAT SOUNDS SMART BUT IS ROOTED IN THE WRONG KINGDOM AND IS POWERLESS TO PRODUCE REAL FRUIT.

This moment - right now - is about acknowledging who you are before God and partnering with the work the Holy Spirit is doing in you. This moment is NOT about shame, it's about re-alignment with your true identity and destiny. Remember, the Earth is literally groaning in eager anticipation of YOU - one of God's most incredible gifts to Earth - the curse-breaker, ambassador of reconciliation, Kingdom of Heaven builder, son of the King of Kings. Your mandate on the earth is to be an amazing water-walking, sight-giving, fish-and-bread-multiplying, demon-crushing, incredible king.

You're valuable and significant because of what Jesus did for you and what Jesus says about you. You're a family member of the King of Kings. You're not defined by your past failure or your current skill-set. Your success, possessions, social status, wealth, and good looks didn't make you, nor will the loss of these things break you.

The earth is waiting for you to embrace your true identity. Heaven is waiting to give you your inheritance. The Holy Spirit is eager to teach you how to build an abundant life and how to govern well. Are you ready? You can begin as soon as you like.

Chapter 11

KRINO

Do not judge so that you will not be judged.

2 "For in the way you judge, you will be judged; and by your standard of measure, it will be measured to you.

3 "Why do you look at the speck that is in your brother's eye, but do not notice the log that is in your own eye?

4 "Or how can you say to your brother, 'Let me take the speck out of your eye,' and behold, the log is in your own eye?

5 "You hypocrite, first take the log out of your own eye, and then you will see clearly to take the speck out of your brother's eye.

—MATTHEW 7:1–5 (NAS)

You've probably heard the "judge not lest ye be judged" passage above a hundred times. Even non-believers know and quote this portion of scripture readily in our modern culture.

What I didn't know was that the specific word Jesus uses for "judge" is the Greek word "krino". I had never heard that word, much less knew its meaning, until my friend and mentor Keith revealed it to me as a cornerstone of the above passage. So I started investigating.

Krino is a Greek word typically used in a legal context meaning "to judge" or, more explicitly, to condemn, avenge, damn, sentence, or levy a punishment against. Yikes. No wonder Jesus warns against this! In this passage, Jesus pokes at one of the favorite sacred cows of the Jewish ruling class - passing judgment. Pharisees of this era had perfected the art of using the law like a club to condemn people and elevate themselves. Is it so different in the Church today? Today Christians blinded by the spirit of religion have inadvertently taken up the same mantle and, like modern day Pharisees, "club" people with the gospel of politics, gospel of good behavior, or gospel of condemnation, and misrepresent the grace-filled Gospel of Jesus Christ - but I digress.

This passage is not a mysterious parable with multiple meanings or subject to varied interpretations. This was neither cryptic nor coy. Jesus boldly warns against "*krino-ing*" others "*lest we be krino-ed*". He goes one step further to say that the measure with which I "*krino*" others is the measure by which I am "*krino-ed*". In a nutshell - what goes around comes around. You reap what you sow. I like it. Golden Rule-esque. Simple words to live by.

One problem... We exist in a culture - whether Christian or non-Christian - that krinos people all the time. It's easy to do. Too easy. It comes about as naturally as breathing and thinking about sex. Some Christian traditions have even spiritualized and celebrate judging people under the guise of "discernment". But as my dad likes to say, "You can't put lipstick on a pig and make it pretty."

Krino is a demon and, besides its ugly cousins Bitterness and Anger, one of the more insidious demons it loves to introduce us to is Victim. Victim is the most subtle and cunning one in the group. As we've explored in previous chapters, people who come under Victim's spell view the world, and people in it, through victim-colored glasses where everyone is out to get them. If we agree with Victim, then the bully's Bitterness and Anger jump into the conversation, giving us spiteful language with which to make declarations of condemnation over our villains. Does this sound familiar? Sadly, I've said all these things and more.

- "That guy's a jerk for cutting me off in traffic."
- "That person meant to hurt me with that comment."
- "That guy is a slacker."
- "My boss is a clueless tyrant."
- "That family is messed up"
- "That guy is a weirdo."
- "I knew things would never work out."
- "Those people judge me all the time."
- "My coworker is a total space-waster."
- "Why me?"
- "My former business associates are crooks."
- "Those people are arrogant."
- "These people are hypocrites."
- "Those people are bad parents."
- "That group is racist."
- "This group is lazy."
- "Those politicians are incompetent liars and cheats."
- "That person makes me so angry."
- And on, and on, and on.....

Did you notice that each of the above statements is a declaration of fact? And most of them are about the other person. And most of them are qualitative assessments that we couldn't possibly KNOW about that person. Are they REALLY a "jerk, hypocrite, slacker, crook... etc.?". By what or whose definition? You get the idea?

My experiences of people I know well are not adequate to allow me to make definitive qualitative declarations about their character, intentions, motives, and identity - much less people I've never met! And yet we find it easy to slip into this seat of judgment. The 24 hour news cycle and talk show hosts speculate wildly with endless commentary, spinning up narratives that may or may not be accurate, and krino effortlessly rolls off their tongues in opinions disguised as facts, which we repeat like parrots, at the coffee shop, at church, work, and throughout our environment till it is saturated with krino. Have we ever stopped to listen to the tone of the narrative? Does anyone wonder who is actually speaking? Does it "sound" like Holy Spirit, or our enemy? I'd suggest that regardless of the content, the tone is how you detect which spirit is speaking. Don't be fooled by content that aligns with your worldview. Remember that Satan used Scripture to temp Jesus, and the Pharisees enslaved all of Israel in a corrupt religious system using the Torah. The Devil knows the "right" answers too.

MY EXPERIENCES OF PEOPLE I KNOW WELL ARE NOT ADEQUATE TO ALLOW ME TO MAKE DEFINITIVE QUALITATIVE DECLARATIONS ABOUT THEIR CHARACTER, INTENTIONS, MOTIVES, AND IDENTITY - MUCH LESS PEOPLE I'VE NEVER MET!

It's funny. You'd think people who are caught in this cycle would feel better about themselves, being the only smart, caring, charming, intelligent, conscientious people in the world. Right? Wrong. When we take the bait and sit in judgment over others, we get caught in Krino's cleverly disguised trap. Remember? The measure by which I judge is the measure by which I am judged. Jesus doesn't warn us about this because it's not "nice" to judge people. He warns us not to put others in the prison of our judgment because in doing so we voluntarily step into our own prison of judgment and our enemy is a ruthless jailer.

Krino is brutal. It's what motivates a mob to drag a woman who has been caught in adultery into the street, naked and shamed, and in blind rage screams for stones to be hurled at her head until she's dead. It exposes without mercy and thrusts its victim into the court of public opinion while it relishes the stoning about to ensue. Fortunately, Jesus is not like us. He's there to hold back the blood-thirsty hypocrites and offer her grace.

> *John 8:1–11 (NLT): Jesus returned to the Mount of Olives, 2 but early the next morning he was back again at the Temple. A crowd soon gathered, and he sat down and taught them. 3 As he was speaking, the teachers of religious law and the Pharisees brought a woman who had been caught in the act of adultery. They put her in front of the crowd.*
>
> *4 "Teacher," they said to Jesus, "this woman was caught in the act of adultery. 5 The law of Moses says to stone her. What do you say?"*
>
> *6 They were trying to trap him into saying something they could use against him, but Jesus stooped down and wrote in the dust with his finger. 7 They kept demanding an answer, so he stood up again and said, "All right, but let the one who has never sinned throw the first stone!" 8 Then he stooped down again and wrote in the dust.*
>
> *9 When the accusers heard this, they slipped away one by one, beginning with the oldest, until only Jesus was left in the middle of the crowd with the woman. 10 Then Jesus stood up again and said to the woman, "Where are your accusers? Didn't even one of them condemn you?"*
>
> *11 "No, Lord," she said.*
>
> *And Jesus said, "Neither do I. Go and sin no more."*

Krino is critical. I know this firsthand because, in the past, judging people came naturally to me. Except I never called it judgment. I called it something more spiritual, like discernment or wisdom. I would sit in my legalistic Christian circles criticizing politicians, church leaders, neighbors, shady business people, bad parents, addicts, rich people, poor people, and on and on. It involved eloquent, self-righteous rants, snap judgments and sweeping generalizations about the "Why's and How's" of large groups of people and their broken-down lives. It involved "krino" without context, without compassion, and with no intention of learning the facts or investing in the people who were the target. It was a sport where people were hunted down the minute they failed, or even faltered. Harsh, critical words were bullets fired at people not present to defend themselves. And after a calculated intellectual assassination, I'd permanently mount their head like a trophy on my wall of judgment. And there, in my mind, they'd hang, without even knowing it... permanently fixed in the same "pose" in my mind, forever judged. Perhaps I'm not the only one?

I'm truly so sad that I was so blind, and so locked up in my own Krino penitentiary for so long. At the heart of my Krino of others was an unspoken declaration of krino over the person I judge the most, ironically, me. It was a spiritually toxic curse, a trap that lured me in and tried to destroy me.

Fortunately for all of us, our King offers a lifeline to help people like me escape Krino's grasp. At the heart of God's view of His creation is the profound value He holds for people. Jesus hanging on a cross is a God's declaration of worth and value over every human being that will ring throughout eternity.

If you question if God values you, or even likes you, ask yourself, in an honest moment, if you've ever truly gotten what you deserved. Ask yourself if you've ever received the DUE penalty for your bad thoughts or actions. Sure, you've paid the price for bad decisions now and then. I'm not talking about speeding tickets. I'm asking have you paid the DUE price for the horrific thoughts you've had or the terrible things you've done. Think about it. The absence of immediate punishment for our sins is the active hand of God holding back cosmic justice - which He created.

I used to think that mercy and grace were wimpy and passive. Now I think of them as a sea wall holding back the violent crashing waves of consequence we deserve. I see Jesus with His hand on Satan's throat, choking him and saying, "SHUT YOUR MOUTH DEVIL! YOU

WILL NO LONGER ACCUSE MY BROTHERS AND SISTERS, DECLARE THEIR GUILT, AND SCRATCH AND SCRAPE FOR THEIR SOULS. THEY BELONG TO ME." It's the same Jesus that rescued the woman caught in adultery, and the same Jesus that scorned the Pharisees, and the same Jesus that rebuked the wind and the waves.

Old mindsets and familiar spirits can be a bitch to get rid of. As a young believer, I wrestled with Krino and critical judgments constantly! But Holy Spirit has graciously, and consistently worn down the hard edges of my weak character and given me new glasses through which to view his world and the people He loves. These glasses help me see like He sees.

New glasses = better judgments. Instead of seeing the worst, I'm learning to look for the best, and a new inner monologue is emerging.

Instead of, "*That guy's a jerk for cutting me off in traffic*", I now often wonder if there is an emergency, or if they're dealing with a stressful situation. Maybe they didn't see me, or maybe they just like to drive crazy. The point is, my initial reaction doesn't have to devolve into a critical snap judgment and a curse against them that robs MY joy and inheritance as a king.

Likewise, instead of asking, "*Why me*?", I now often ask Holy Spirit to give me insight, wisdom, and eternal perspective beyond what I can see and comprehend now. Joseph could have asked, "*Why me*?" When his brothers sold him into slavery, but God was with him, offering perspective, and ultimately, he saved an entire nation and his brothers from starvation. Stephen could have easily asked "*Why me?*" but his intimacy with Holy Spirit enabled him to literally see God *while* he was being stoned. Stephen's martyrdom became a turning point for Saul, a terrorist, who later became Paul, a Spirit filled ambassador for the Gospel and author of a significant portion of the New Testament. In the same way, Paul could have easily asked, "*Why me?*" when he was beaten, imprisoned, or shipwrecked. Instead, we routinely see him respond with eternal perspective and manifest fruits of the Spirit that prove his connection with Holy Spirit.

Don't misunderstand me. I'm not saying they were perfect, and obviously neither are we. As one of my physical trainers often says, "we're a work in progress and a masterpiece at the same time." When I'm tired, stressed, or not guarding my heart, I can quickly revert to seeing the worst in people and making snap judgments. In these moments, Krino is an unwelcome companion who sneaks into my car and rides shot-gun with me through life, reminding me how lazy, stupid, incompetent, mean, and selfish everyone else in my world is.

To be a good king, we must become masters at detecting His voice and ejecting him the instant he speaks. Krino is not to have any influence over a king's inner thought life, much less his mouth. If Krino corrupts a king's thoughts, he becomes vulnerable to the ugly cousins I referenced before - Bitterness, Anger, Victim, and others. And we all know that kings trapped by these demons do NOT represent the King of Kings or his Kingdom well.

If you struggle with krino or judgmental mindsets - what do you do? The good news is that Holy Spirit is already at work in us to set us free from this prison and we live in an ocean of His grace that empowers us to grow, free from, wait for it... judgment. So relax, and settle into the process.

Trials.

Yes, we're talking about trials... again.... I would never have put it together on my own that God's recipe for revealing old "krino" mindsets in me was a good ole' fashioned hardship or two. In previous chapters, we've discovered tools to help navigate trials and difficult seasons. My family and I have lived through two distinctly difficult seasons in the past 20 years. These seasons stretched my family and marriage further than I thought possible. And by God's grace, a lot of "junk" was forced to the surface and healed as each trial revealed my breaking point.

Full disclosure. I'm writing this on my iPad hooked to my wi-fi sitting in my chair as I look out at the beautiful western mountain ranges of Northern California. In the context of human history, as a Western American Christian, I am better off than 99.9% of people who've ever lived on Earth. This is not intended to bring shame on me or anyone like me, just a healthy perspective.

It's healthy for us to appreciate that our version of "hardships" would be like a fluffy vanilla ice-cream cone for many of our fellow kings around the world who would gladly trade places with us. The mere fact that I can sit here and write this book while I sip coffee indicates how far removed I am from the horrors others around the world have endured. Recently, I was privileged to attend a meeting where we listened to missionaries from Afghanistan tell us about the atrocities the Taliban are carrying out against our fellow kings and queens there. It was a good perspective. It stirred in me a passion to pray and motivation to help.

In these perspective-aligning moments, it's important to not allow shame to overwhelm us or it can create a sort of "survivor's guilt" that prevents us from honestly acknowledging our own trials, pain and disappointments. For me, I can easily recall that familiar voice of my grandmother ringing in my mind... "other people have it worse, so put on a happy face and be grateful". While there is value in having perspective, there is something inauthentic, and frankly, emotionally and mentally dangerous about sweeping your emotional pain or trauma under the rug. Unlike physical wounds, emotional wounds don't heal themselves, they just go underground and grow.

UNLIKE PHYSICAL WOUNDS, EMOTIONAL WOUNDS DON'T HEAL THEMSELVES, THEY JUST GO UNDERGROUND AND GROW.

Kings understand this delicate balance between perspective, gratitude, and dealing honestly with the pain and trauma of their trials. They know how to be kind to themselves in the process and know that they had no control over where they were born, their family of origin, or their particular Enneagram, DISC, and Myers-Briggs personality type.

Whether born into a royal family or a slum, your context is significant and your journey with the Lord is unique to you. Deal with that journey honestly and be present with Him. He's not mad at you because you're not stronger or further along. His path for healing and progress for you isn't always to focus on those less fortunate and the denial of your problems in favor of theirs. He's patiently waiting to help you confront your giants. Whether they're big or small by world's standards - they're important to Him, and He is committed to empowering you to defeat every one of them.

I won't bore you with details of my individual trials themselves. Let me just say that they included betrayal, scandal, abandonment, loss, financial devastation, sickness, lying, stealing, depression, addiction, etc. You know... the usual stuff.

As we discussed in previous chapters, I'd suggest that you'll never know the weakness of your character without the fire of trials. Trials publish our weaknesses, one volume after another. And because kings need to be strong, Holy Spirit uses our trials as training for reigning.

Being on the receiving end of trials tempts you to feel abandoned and afraid. As a young king, I found it easiest to turn to many unhealthy coping mechanisms when the fire got hot. I drank. I escaped into pornography. I bought stuff I didn't need. I blamed others. I worked too much. In short, I ran away. I tried to hide. I tried to escape.

In extreme moments, I would launch into Job-esque temper tantrums directed at the ceiling. I recall these moments, first in the house on Spruce and in my office, in my car on my way home from work, and in the red house, then in the house in Texas, then the trailer, then the apartment again - yeah, I've thrown a lot of temper tantrums over the years.

I kicked and screamed and complained and played the victim. I know He heard it, but He was, for the most part, silent. In His mercy, He never flamed back at me the way I've flamed at Him. And there is a reason for that. His current response to sin, and the occasional rant from one of his beloved sons, is endless grace.

But grace doesn't necessarily mean immediate deliverance and resolution of circumstances. As we've discussed, our King is NOT a helicopter parent. Trials have a job to do and Holy Spirit is committed to a job well done. Every time I wanted to tap out, He'd drag me back into the ring for another round of training. He wouldn't let me quit the healing process. He wouldn't let me escape the desert, the wilderness, the dark night of the soul. And why would He? In my most honest and earnest prayers, I'd asked for Him to change me and make me more like Jesus! Of course, when I made that request, I thought that simply meant going to seminary or something simple like that. Little did I know much of the training would be enduring hardships, and surrendering to the training process over, and over, and over again.

Let me be clear, every trial is different, and even the causes can be different. Sometimes trials are an overt attack from our enemy and our correct response as a king is to bind him, tear down his works, and frustrate his plans.

In other seasons, trials can serve as a gentle reminder from a loving Father who doesn't want me to play with poisonous mindsets or flirt with fire. For me, my propensity to be critical and embrace Krino - like a Pharisee - was unhealthy and my King allowed the fire of trials to refine that garbage out of me and set me free. It was for my good. It was His lovingkindness, and it worked. It burned away pride and arrogance so that I can now weigh situations with care and see people with empathy. Instead of casually dismissing people in a momentary judgment, I approach people with compassion, seeking to know their story, motives, and pain. My own experiences of financial devastation helped me gain an appreciation for those who can't make ends meet. My own struggles with addiction have allowed me to empathize with the addicts I meet and counsel with. My experience of being led into a wilderness with no support system has prompted me to extend hospitality to people around me who feel alone and displaced. It's finally making sense to me, not just philosophically, but at the gut level, why Jesus said "judge not, lest ye be judged." You see, it's His kindness that leads us all to repentance.

Kindness is unmistakable and amazing, especially when it appears in places where you least expect it. I've always been blown away by people who can offer grace and hospitality to others when they are in the "fire". I've sat with people in Palestinian refugee camps with up to 30 people living in a 20' x 20' room with a thatch roof and dirt floor with a small cookstove and one or two pots to cook meals. No toilet. No privacy. No basic sanitary supplies or toiletries. No place to bury their dead but the landfill they live in. And worst of all, no hope of ever getting out. These are unimaginably difficult circumstances, so much so that it was difficult to keep my mind from simply shutting down from shock. For me, the sheer exhaustion of even processing that level of despair and the darkness leaves me somewhere between numb and hopeless.

Yet, astoundingly, I routinely found a generous spirit and authentic joy in the lives of believers living in dark places like this. How can this be???? I was utterly baffled by it. In this environment, I would have expected words of bitterness and anger to ring in my ears just like the stench of feces and decay stung my nostrils. Instead, I routinely found the "fragrant bouquet" of hospitality and grace. It was shocking and profound - the essence of the Kingdom.

In my world of excess and abundance, my first instinct is to "krino" everyone into oblivion. However, in their world of abject poverty, their first instinct is to graciously embrace me, an entitled American "tourist", who was there one day and was gone the next. Their toilet is a public ditch outside their house that breeds disease and stinks, while I can choose from one of several toilets inside my house that contain more clean, running water than they will have access to in a week.

They should judge me. They should "krino" me for my Western

American laziness, lack of gratitude, superiority complex, ego-centric obliviousness to the world's problems, apathy, hypocrisy, etc. etc. etc.

Instead, I was given gifts. In one home, I received a valuable hand made blanket. In another I was an honored guest, invited to share a meal that cost one month's wages. I was even invited to a wedding celebration usually only attended by close family. I was the recipient of profound acts of hospitality and generosity from impoverished people who loved and did not judge. They are the true children of God; kings and queens who reveal His Kingdom as they walk out Jesus' mission. When you see that up close, it's profound and humbling. No, it's stupefying. His kindness, displayed by these kings and queens, is what ultimately led me to a profound repentance from all forms of krino in my life.

Don't misunderstand, some less gracious folks heckled us and threw rocks at us from time to time as well. Poverty and crises obviously also breed bitterness and anger. But those who find the capacity to love and not "krino" stick in my mind like a splinter and I can't forget them. They are drenched in fragrant oil of Heaven.

THE PUNCHLINE

My trials have humbled me. Those who face more harsh trials than mine inspire me and give me perspective. They encourage me to keep fighting the good fight to see this world through the eyes of love and to remain free from the prison of judgment.

My trials are birthing in me, genuine love, long-suffering, perseverance, and empathy. They are producing humility and a counter-intuitive confidence in God's goodness. They are producing self-control that enables me to hold my tongue instead of using it as a whip. They are opportunities to draw closer to my heavenly Abba, let Him comfort me, and let Him be my strength and not reasons to lash out at Him in my pain - at least on my best days.

True kings think differently about God. For a true king, God is not an angry, disconnected Father waiting for them to make one mistake so He can judge them, kill them, and get it over with. He doesn't view human beings as an annoying cosmic mistake that He has to put up with until He can wipe the slate clean and try again.

Kings are good at seeing God correctly. 1 Corintians 13 says that love keeps no record of wrongs. In 1st John 4, we learn God is love, therefore, for those of us who've received and accepted his forgiveness, God is not keeping a record of our wrongs. Romans 8:1 further states there is no more condemnation for us who are in Christ, which by definition means that there must no longer be anything in us to condemn. Right? Doesn't the justice and holiness of God require that? He hates sin; He loves us. Therefore, it is impossible for Him to see us as guilty of any sin. He sees us only as righteous and holy because we are in Christ.

THIS IS HOW GOD FREES US FROM THE BONDAGE OF JUDGMENT. HE'S NOT KEEPING SCORE, SO WE DON'T HAVE TO EITHER, FOR OURSELVES, AND ESPECIALLY NOT FOR OTHERS.

It says our wrongs (sins) are thrown as far as the East is from the West. In another passage, it says that they are thrown into the deepest ocean and remembered no more. This is how God frees us from the bondage of judgment. He's not keeping score, so we don't have to either, for ourselves, and especially not for others. He's not judging our sin anymore because He dealt with that once and for all in Jesus' death and resurrection.

Now He's judging our goodness through our NEW life which is in Christ. As new creations in Christ, we have the amazing capacity to speak and create along with Holy Spirit. We've transitioned from objects of judgment to beloved sons. I can imagine Him smiling whenever we create, emote, observe, discern, wonder, and believe because in these moments we resemble Him. I see Him swell with pride and affection even more when we bless, offer grace, show kindness and extend mercy. I think these moments make Him downright giddy. These moments are evidence that the "apples have not fallen so far from the tree".

The point is that He's focused on the good, the potential, and measuring us for an imperishable Heaven-suit and a glorious inheritance of blessings He's painstakingly chosen to give us now and in the age to come. He's preparing good gifts and wants us to ask Him for them. And judgment of others is just holding us back from receiving all that He wants to give.

Don't believe me? Still have doubts about His goodness toward you? Still wonder if He's really keeping score or if you have to earn His love and approval? Perhaps the next few verses from this same sermon Jesus preached will convince you.

> *Matthew 7:7–12 (NAS): Ask, and it will be given to you; seek, and you will find; knock, and it will be opened to you.*
>
> *8 "For everyone who asks receives, and he who seeks finds, and to him who knocks it will be opened.*
>
> *9 "Or what man is there among you who, when his son asks for a loaf, will give him a stone?*
>
> *10 "Or if he asks for a fish, he will not give him a snake, will he?*
>
> *11 "If you then, being evil, know how to give good gifts to your children, how much more will your Father who is in heaven give what is good to those who ask Him!*
>
> *12 "In everything, therefore, treat people the same way you want them to treat you, for this is the Law and the Prophets.*

Kings, you know what to do. Take inventory of your thoughts about others. Be ruthlessly honest about your tendency to allow Krino a voice in your life. Holy Spirit is ready and eager to set you free. Let's do it.

Chapter 12

THE MAKER AND HIS MAKERS

If you're relying exclusively on your intellect to solve problems, then you're simply not accessing your highest skill sets in Christ that God has given you to navigate challenges and express God's glory through your creativity. The Scriptures illustrate in story after story how much Holy Spirit loves to show up in the details. Just read the specific instructions Moses receives about how to construct the Tabernacle in Exodus 26 and you'll come to understand how much our King is concerned about the details. It makes sense, right? Imagine a chef who didn't care about the presentation of their meal. Imagine a woodworker who didn't care about the finish or the joints in their creation. Sloppiness and shortcuts are not the way of our King and we instinctively know it. If you doubt me, just think back to your own reaction the last time you're in the presence of something that was beautifully crafted. Were you impressed? Did it take your breath away? Did you marvel at the attention to detail? Kings, this is the kind of reaction the Earth is supposed to have at the works of OUR hands, whether in writing a book, painting, woodworking, driving a truck, writing up a loan, selling cars, or running a restaurant.

There is an unhealthy mindset that has permeated the Church in the past several decades that encourages the children of God to shy away from the spotlight, to avoid praise, and to deflect any attention in some effort to avoid becoming prideful. This is utter nonsense. As one of my favorite mentors and preachers likes to say, the painting gives no glory to the artist by telling an admirer to "look away" or by downplaying its beauty. On the contrary, the painting should call out to everyone, "Come! Look at me! And see the incredible talent and love of the Artist who made me!" Excellence is a hallmark of the Kingdom, and it is an ongoing pursuit of kings who belong to Heaven.

THE SPIRIT OF GOD IS THE MASTER CRAFTSMAN. HE KNOWS EVERYTHING, HAS INFINITE POWER TO DO ANYTHING, AND LIVES INSIDE YOU.

Exodus 31:1–11 (NLT): Then the Lord said to Moses, 2 "Look, I
have specifically chosen Bezalel son of Uri, grandson of Hur, of the
tribe of Judah. 3 I have filled him with the Spirit of God, giving
him great wisdom, ability, and expertise in all kinds of crafts. 4
He is a master craftsman, expert in working with gold, silver, and
bronze. 5 He is skilled in engraving and mounting gemstones and
in carving wood. He is a master at every craft!

6 "And I have personally appointed Oholiab son of Ahisamach, of the tribe of Dan, to be his assistant. Moreover, I have given special skill to all the gifted craftsmen so they can make all the things I have commanded you to make:

7 the Tabernacle;

the Ark of the Covenant;

the Ark's cover—the place of atonement;

all the furnishings of the Tabernacle;

8 the table and its utensils;

the pure gold lampstand with all its accessories;

the incense altar;

9 the altar of burnt offering with all its utensils;

the washbasin with its stand;

10 the beautifully stitched garments—the sacred garments for Aaron the priest, and the garments for his sons to wear as they minister as priests;

11 the anointing oil;

the fragrant incense for the Holy Place.

The craftsmen must make everything as I have commanded you."

The Spirit of God is the Master craftsman. He knows everything, has infinite power to do anything, and lives inside you. As a rule, we should be over-asking, over-seeking, and overly attentive to what he's thinking and saying about every detail of our life. A dear friend of mine who used to lead the prayer ministry at a church where I lead worship used to tell me he would even ask Holy Spirit what shirt he should wear when he woke up. I think that's the profile of a king. One who doesn't partition off ANY portion of their life, but freely opens a dialogue with Holy Spirit about every detail, and then waits to listen to the answer.

Some days there will be clear answers, other days there may be silence, but the point is that we care what He's thinking and acknowledge His authority over everything in our life, even the details.

The above passage is the first place in Scripture that describes someone being "filled" with the Holy Spirit, and notice that it doesn't say he shook, fell on the floor, spoke in tongues, laughed, had a dream, vision, wrote a book, preached, or anything like that. Before you think I'm being all judgey let me set the record straight. I love all those things, and have done them all, and love every moment I spend in the presence of God where His power manifests physically in me and others in wild and beautiful ways.

But what I find fascinating about this is that he was filled with the Spirit and was given the supernatural capacity and skills to do work in a particular way that had never been done before, and presumably he had not learned from any other human.

This brings the Holy Spirit, His gifts, power, and manifestations OUT of the realm of high-church experience and into the practical realm of men who wear boots to work and get their hands dirty. This is what I love about this passage. I love that our Heavenly Father is a worker, a creative craftsman. One who loves to show off His craftsmanship and creativity expressed through tangible work as much as He loves to be revealed through wisdom and revelation that He gives teachers and ministers. Both/and. Evangelist AND a tent maker. Savior AND a carpenter. Being and doing. Receiving freely and working diligently. I love this about God. Our challenge as kings is to discern what is required for the season by bringing Holy Spirit into the discussion as our starting place.

In the Winter of 2009 I had a dream about a machine. In my dream, I was with one of my old college professors and we were standing in a line outside a store waiting to enter. It was cold and snow fell softly, glinting in the warm glow of the streetlights. People in line were chatting and laughing in their stocking caps and winter coats, eagerly waiting to enter the store and buy whatever was being served up inside the popular establishment. Behind me, the line seemed to extend for several blocks. Before long, we stood directly in front of the large glass window at the front of the store and through a misty snow-glazed window, I could see a machine. It was a simple-looking machine about the size of a small deep freeze, but black, with a stainless steel top, and it had two long vertical glass tubes that rose elegantly from the top. Inside the tubes were small brown beans floating and bouncing.

At that moment I awoke and somehow I knew that was a machine that I was going to build, and it was a coffee roaster. Mind you, up till this moment, the sum total of my experience with coffee had been drinking it. My wife and I both loved coffee, but we weren't fanatics about it like some. However, over the coming months and years, we would become full-blown, unapologetic, coffee nerds.

BOTH/AND. EVANGELIST AND A TENT MAKER. SAVIOR AND A CARPENTER. BEING AND DOING. RECEIVING FREELY AND WORKING DILIGENTLY.

I believe our King looks to partner with His kings. Like a good Father, He loves to see us discover our inheritance and destiny that He's lovingly hidden along our path. It's like a divine scavenger hunt where He provides dreams, Holy Spirit prompts and words, scripture, and many other clues that point us toward our promised abundant life and Kingdom assignments.

Over the next year, I investigated all manner of coffee roasting equipment, methods, trends, and schools of thought. My wife and I attended Coffee Fest in NYC and experienced the latest and greatest in the exploding world of artisan coffee roasting. We experimented with different brewing methods and roast profiles. We connected with coffee brokers and farmers in Tanzania, Haiti, South America, Indonesia, and others. We started roasting coffee with small roasters to experiment and learn our craft. Soon we were using multiple little roasters to sell artisan coffee to the local college, to local coffee shops and specialty grocery stores in the area. My wife was the roast master, but it was clear we needed a bigger machine to keep up with demand.

I still marvel at how God works. I was a general studies major in college with an emphasis on religion, philosophy, music, and business. I didn't study physics and was not a craftsman who could build a coffee roaster. But I started the process anyway. My first roaster prototype was pretty rough. It looked like some kind of NASA satellite had crashed in my backyard. But in true miraculous fashion, I built it inside of 3 months and it worked nearly perfectly on the first day of use.

I praised God for His grace on the project and vowed that the next one was going to look like the beautiful piece of machinery I'd seen in my dream...

One door after another continued to open for us and before we knew it, we were so busy roasting coffee; we had little time for anything else. At one point, Jess told me we needed a break, and I agreed. We took our three small children and went on a brief vacation to get some downtime. While we were away, our largest customer, a local coffee shop, contacted us and needed to reorder because they'd sold out over the weekend. As we talked, it became clear that we could not keep up with their growing needs and Holy Spirit dropped a word into my spirit. "Build them the coffee roaster you saw in your dream and put it in their front window."

So I'd partnered with a friend of mine who owned and operated a metal fabrication shop to draw up plans. Rusty was, and still is, a consummate craftsman and builds beautiful machines used by hot rod enthusiasts around the world to bend and fabricate metal. In his free time, he also builds and races top fuel drag race cars and also is a fellow drummer in our church worship band. Rusty is a king who knows and loves the King of Kings with his whole being. With his help, the next one emerged as a true work of art.

In record time, we completed the build and installed the finished product. All glory to God. The coffee shop at the time was run by a friend of ours who began studying artisan coffee roasting and within the first several months he had transformed the sleepy coffee shop into a bustling hot spot where the coffee was known for excellence and the experience was amazing. You could walk in, request a bag of your preferred single-origin coffee, or even your own special blend, and 12-15 minutes later walk out with a warm bag of freshly roasted whole bean coffee.

Curtis, our friend who became the roast master, even had local groups request organized tours to come and see him roast the coffee.

The bottom line impact to the business was savings of over $30,000 the first year reduced COGS because instead of purchasing roasted coffee, the shop now bought green coffee in jute sacks at less than half the price. The novelty and ambiance of the shop were magical and the relationships we built with coffee growers to purchase direct and provide fair prices for their green coffee put more money in their pocket.

In a small dream about a simple machine, the King of Kings had deposited a gift into the Earth to bless one of his sons, a coffee shop owner, a small town, and coffee farmers around the globe. This is how the Kingdom works. This is how God manifests His glory in and through the Earth.

Today, innovators like Elon Musk and Mark Zuckerberg get a lot of press for their vision and creativity and rightfully so. Romans 11:29 tells us that the gifts and callings of God are irrevocable, which means whether or not you honor the King with your life, you were given a gift and calling, and you can step into it. We see this in the entertainment industry all the time with particularly gifted musicians, actors, and various other entertainers. The fact is that you have been given a gift. Perhaps you have a particular musical skill, or an Einstein-esque knack for mathematics and physics, or perhaps you're an inventor like my father. Regardless of whether you ever acknowledge God or honor Him with your gift, He still gave it to you and is elated to see you use it. You can't get away from the reality that in using your gift, you glorify Him as the creator and giver of that gift. So I love to see Elon and his contemporaries explore new realms of what is possible. Regardless of whether or not they give God glory, I do.

But it hurts my heart to realize that the sons of God, who have been given access to the revelation and wisdom of Heaven, are conspicuously absent from the front lines of human progress. Where are the skilled craftsmen, the artisans, researchers, artists, those who have intimacy with Holy Spirit and who are supernaturally empowered to subdue and steward the Earth and advance humankind through the creativity of our King? Whether you're a minister, farmer, banker, or fisherman, the Holy Spirit wants to infuse you with a supernatural wisdom, passion and energy so that YOUR inspired work displays HIS glory and majesty to such a degree that the world stands in awe of His greatness.

HONEST REFLECTION

It's been a few years since the coffee roaster dream, and I'd like to tell you I stewarded that dream and season well, but honestly, I didn't. The roaster worked flawlessly for over two years and roasted over seven thousand pounds of coffee with no maintenance or breakdowns. I started work on another prototype that could roast larger batches and incorporated a few other design improvements, but the cares of life, money, time, and a growing family slowly choked out the dream and the pressure to focus on a "normal" job soon eclipsed the dream to build a coffee roaster business. The original roaster eventually broke down, and I simply didn't have the time to repair or replace it. With no funding, and no time, the fire for the dream dimmed to a faint ember.

As a young king, I didn't recognize this as a test, but in hindsight, I know it was. The god of Mammon - money - was establishing a blockade around the roaster to contain its divine effect and to squash the Kingdom glory it was intended to exhibit. At the time, I didn't understand my identity, my inheritance, and my placement in Christ as one who has been given all things. So I succumbed to the inferior "reality" that I could not accomplish the dream God had placed in my heart because of my lack of resources. Mammon is a demon that attempts to control the resources and economies of the Earth and has established himself as a gatekeeper with the power to promote or block endeavors based on his ability to control the flow of money. Mammon thrives on promoting the earthbound mindset that your dream is only viable if you have enough money and time to make it happen, and then he stands as lord over those resources, enslaving all who come to him. If you negotiate your dreams with Mammon, he will force you to compromise the purity of the dream and will castrate its Kingdom purpose.

Kings, Mammon isn't funding the dreams that Heaven has deposited in your heart. He's not writing checks to you and me so we can manifest the glory of his archenemy and advance the Kingdom of Heaven. On the contrary, he's attempting to choke out those dreams. His objective is to systematically enslave you to "grinding it out" inside an Earthly system that pays you as little as possible while it exploits and extracts as much of your time, talents and abilities as it can. His system is built on promoting scarcity and fear instead of generosity, abundance, and the infinite resources that are the hallmark of our King of Kings and His Kingdom.

IF YOU NEGOTIATE YOUR DREAMS WITH MAMMON, HE WILL FORCE YOU TO COMPROMISE THE PURITY OF THE DREAM AND WILL CASTRATE ITS KINGDOM PURPOSE.

It's critical for kings to mature past the notion that money is any sort of gatekeeper into your divine destiny in the Kingdom. Remember, you serve the King who produced a miraculous catch of fish for his disciples the first day they met. He's the same King that caught a fish with coins in its mouth to pay his and his friend's taxes. He's the same King that multiplied fish and loaves to feed thousands with no money at all. He's the same King that turned water into wine and who routinely bypassed the systems and principalities of the first and second realms that are ruled by our enemy. He can invade time and space with resources that can literally appear out of thin air, and He exercises supreme authority over all natural laws. Ask the Israelites who were liberated from Egypt by miraculous plagues, and who were given manna and quail every day for 40 years in the wilderness, and whose clothes and sandals never wore out, if our King can provide resources for your journey - with or without money. I think they'd all agree that He can.

The true reality is NOT that you lack the money or time to do the will of our King - regardless of what your schedule or bank account tell you. The truth is that our King has assignments for us and He has provision for us to accomplish those assignments. It may not come in a common currency of Earth like money or time or a powerful network of friends and associates. It may come in peculiar and very unexpected ways, like we often read in Scriptures. The point is that for kings, lack of resources is NEVER an obstacle to realizing your divine destiny because there is no lack of resources in the Kingdom. Holy Spirit is a reliable guide who will chart the path forward, complete with all the resources we need, if we let Him.

FOR KINGS, LACK OF RESOURCES IS NEVER AN OBSTACLE TO REALIZING YOUR DIVINE DESTINY BECAUSE THERE IS NO LACK OF RESOURCES IN THE KINGDOM.

The coffee roaster dream is still alive even up to this day, again, not because I stewarded it well, but because it started as a dream in my King's heart and He stewards His dreams, and kings, VERY well. He can renew the lost years and even as I write this I'm stirred in my spirit to have a conversation with Holy Spirit about the future of this project. Over time, I've learned that while we may have dropped dreams along the path as we stumble forward through life, Holy Spirit never let them hit the ground. He catches them and waits until we're ready to breathe new life into them.

Perhaps there is a dream in your heart that Holy Spirit wants to revive? Maybe you have a literal dream or vision that you need to take more seriously? Maybe, like me, you started out strong, and His favor was on you, but then you faltered and lost sight of His dream. Holy Spirit can make up for lost time, and He's a genius at fulfilling the plans and purposes of our King.

Kings, you know what to do. This is a good moment to take an inventory. Are you walking in your destiny, or have you settled for a lesser path? No shame, or blame, Holy Spirit doesn't do that. But He will highlight the better path He has for us. When He does, resolve to explore the mystery and possibilities with Him and go all in. He is trustworthy and good and the Earth is waiting for us to put on display the amazing creativity and craftsmanship of our King.

Chapter 13

FLOW

Kings, are you noticing a recurring theme here? Perhaps you're detecting a common thread woven intentionally through nearly every chapter? A key that unlocks your inheritance? As we've explored - at great length - the process for your kingship to emerge involves seasons of refinement in the fire of trials that offer us an invitation to deeper intimacy with our King. In these seasons, we learn to access power beyond ourselves so we can face our giants and win. With every chapter, we're exploring different tools and facets of this central theme.

In this chapter, I want to explore yet another tool Holy Spirit has that empowers us to survive and thrive in the process: Flow. As we've explored, I didn't realize how much of a blind spot this was for me until God revealed it to me many years ago. He continues to develop it further with the help of some good friends right up to this day. I used to think I was living in step with Holy Spirit all the time, but as is always the case, there's more to learn, more intimacy to gain, and more He wants to give us as we seek Him.

We understand how the spirit of religion has duped us into believing that our relationship with God is a programmatic, intellectual, educational process where we read books, learn the theories about God, and assume that we know Him. But by now, it should be obvious that a true relationship with God is experiential, relational, and tangible in the same way every other relationship in your life is. But, as in so many areas of life, our enemy has blinded the minds and hearts of smart people to very simple truths.

For example, smart people understand that reading a book about George Washington doesn't mean you know him and we all accept that as an obvious fact about George Washington. Why? Because he's dead. It doesn't even register in the mind of any sane person that we could have a relationship with George Washington. Instead, we understand that what we're really doing is learning ABOUT George Washington. Yes, Matt, we understand this. What's your point?

My point is that we take this exact approach to learning ABOUT Jesus, and the intellectual result is identical. Don't believe me? The Pharisees knew the Torah, but little good it did them. Jesus stood right before them and they didn't recognize him as the promised Messiah. Instead, they labeled Him a heretic and killed Him. We'd like to think we would behave a lot differently today, but would we really? We've got the rules down, the programs, the worship bands, the behavior, the colleges, seminaries, radio stations and podcasts. We've got commentaries and content generators that stream more information than any time in history. And yet we are bombarded with social statistics that seem to reveal that we're not living the abundant, overcoming life we were promised. I believe this is because relationships are built on experiential encounters, not information.

One facet of connecting with God is definitely reading Scripture, but it's not adequate alone for kings. We need the relationship that comes from connection - heart to heart. We also need to hear His voice as Jesus proclaimed we would in John 10, when He told the people that His sheep know His voice. We need easy dialogue with the Holy Spirit about the practical matters of life, as Jesus said we would have in Luke 12:12 and John 16:13 when He taught His disciples that the Holy Spirit would teach them what to say and would lead them into all truth.

I've never met a believer yet who said, "I don't want to hear from the Holy Spirit" or "I don't want to hear the voice of God". Most of the time, people tell me how frustrated they are because they don't know HOW to hear Him. So how does this process start? A few things I've learned...

You probably don't fully realize, but your inner monologue is anything but "mono". As we've discovered through our exploration of the first, second, and third realms, there are many players that speak as you meditate and ponder in your innermost thoughts. Your brain, your spirit, your body, the Holy Spirit, the Devil, just to name a few. And they don't always speak in words. They can use visions, images, feelings, senses, thoughts, visualizations, among others. Read the Bible and see the variety of ways God speaks. For now, I'd like to unpack a specific blind spot I had in hearing Holy Spirit in hopes that it will help you as you seek to hear Holy Spirit.

You know that small, almost imperceptible voice in your head that you often brush aside, but that sounds like you? That's not always you. That's often the voice of the Holy Spirit. We often think that thoughts light *randomly* on our minds - but let me assure you, they're not always random. And when they rise into *your* conscious mind, they are "*heard*" in the first person and, therefore, use *your* voice. This is because they're happening inside *your* conscious mind. Certainly you can think original thoughts, so often these conscious thoughts are, in fact, just your thoughts. However, it could also be Holy Spirit because, as we know from Scripture, that Holy Spirit is fused together with your Spirit - for eternity. Holy Spirit speaks to you through a hard-line wired directly into your spirit that Paul describes in 1 Corinthians 2:16 when he explains that we have been given the "mind of Christ". That's another way of saying, Christ's thoughts can come into our mind - and do - via the Holy Spirit - which lives in us. Recall that Christ is in Heaven, seated at the right hand of God the Father, and Holy Spirit is presently here on Earth dwelling inside all believers. Also, recall that you're presently seated in Heavenly places with Christ, while your physical body is here. Still tracking? Let me summarize it this way. Christ's physical, glorified, resurrected body ascended to Heaven, and 50 days later, His Spirit came down at Pentecost. Your physical body is here, and your Spirit can ascend to Heaven via the spiritual connection you share with Holy Spirit. Think of it like cable TV or Internet. The connection provides access to an entire world of content, right? Your connection to Holy Spirit provides you access to a superior world of resources, wisdom, glorious beings, and supernatural power. So, yeah, it's a lot better than cable TV or internet. This isn't some far out theory, it's a practical reality.

WHILE INTELLECTUALISM, LOGIC, AND RATIONALE ARE THE NATIVE LANGUAGE OF EARTH, THEY ARE NOT THE NATIVE LANGUAGE OF HEAVEN.

But navigating this reality requires tuning our hearts to hear differently than we used to. While intellectualism, logic, and rationale are the native language of Earth, they are not the native language of Heaven.

And like an old FM radio, tuning out the static so we can hear clearly is an art kings must seek to perfect.

As citizens of the Kingdom of Heaven, kings must not only begin to learn Heaven's native tongue, but seek to make it their first language, and allow "Earth/English/Etc" to become their second language. If this is confusing, you're not alone. Let me explain. The language spoken in Heaven is a spiritual language, and it's fundamentally different and wonderful! Spiritual language is much more than simple linguistics or images that your physical brain can intellectually comprehend and describe as with English.

Honestly, when the Spirit "speaks" and our physical brains are forced to interpret, it can be an awkward struggle to comprehend and communicate. Just read Zecharia's struggle to explain his vision of the lampstand as he dialogues with the angel in Zechariah 4 or listen to Ezekiel describe his visions of wheels within wheels in Ezekiel 1 or John's explanation of what he sees in Revelation.

Paul elaborates on this idea in 1 Corinthians when he says:

> *1 Corinthians 13:9–12 (NLT): Now our knowledge is partial and incomplete, and even the gift of prophecy reveals only part of the whole picture! 10 But when the time of perfection comes, these partial things will become useless.*
>
> *11 When I was a child, I spoke and thought and reasoned as a child. But when I grew up, I put away childish things. 12 Now we see things imperfectly, like puzzling reflections in a mirror, but then we will see everything with perfect clarity. All that I know now is partial and incomplete, but then I will know everything completely, just as God now knows me completely.*

You get the point. Our intellectual minds can only understand part of the picture. Spiritual language is multidimensional and includes prophecy, dreams, visions, pictures, words, thoughts, feelings, knowings, and more - much of which will confound our natural intellectual mind. As Earth-born children, our first language consists mostly of the language of our conscious intellectual mind. Yes, our imaginations and emotions have a "voice" as well, but for many of us, our culture trains from an early age to suppress those "voices" in favor of common sense rational thinking. Until we're born again, we have no awareness or access to the superior Kingdom of our King, much less how to speak or understand the language.

Disclaimer: I know that non-believers have dreams and visions and can hear from God. I know believers whose first encounter with God was a vision or dream and this is documented all throughout scripture as well. Yes, God can break into our world at any time and speak in unmistakable ways. I'm not talking about those moments. I'm talking about tuning our spiritual senses to detect and comprehend what Holy Spirit is saying on an ongoing basis as one of Jesus "sheep" who knows His voice as the John 10:28 passage above states.

My intellectual brain has a strong voice, so, for me, I know that Holy Spirit often has to bypass it with dreams, visions, and "strange" encounters. But the goal for kings is to become fluent in the language of the Spirit so that our brain and its intellectual faculties become subject to, and aligned with, the superior Kingdom and leading of the Spirit. Our passage below illustrates this.

> *Proverbs 3:5–7 (AMP): Lean on, trust in, and be confident in the Lord with all your heart and mind and do not rely on your own insight or understanding.*
>
> *6 In all your ways know, recognize, and acknowledge Him, and He will direct and make straight and plain your paths.*
>
> *7 Be not wise in your own eyes; reverently fear and worship the Lord and turn [entirely] away from evil.*

So we understand the Spirit speaks to us in a language we're learning, and we know He speaks in "not so random" thoughts that light upon our mind. Are there other players speaking? Yes, indeed. Unfortunately, our enemy, the Devil, and his demons, used to be citizens of Heaven as well and as we observe in Jesus' temptation in the wilderness, they know the Bible and they know how to trash talk. They can plant thoughts in your mind, but the good news is that Holy Spirit completely displaced their influence in your Spirit when He came to dwell inside you, and He can help you "hear" the truth above their lies.

Let me share an analogy that may be helpful. I like to think of my mind as the "forum" where I discuss ideas with Holy Spirit. Unfortunately, our enemy will slip in unannounced and hijack the conversation from time to time with thoughts that are destructive. Unfortunately, these also sound like first-person thoughts, so it can be difficult to identify him as the source of these lies at first. As the Bible shows us, Satan is cunning. He often will appeal to our natural mind's affinity for logic, reason, and rational thinking in order to deceive us. Just look at how he speaks to Eve in the garden and Jesus in the wilderness. The arguments he presents make sense to the intellectual mind and were even backed by Scripture! But they're obvious traps meant to steal, kill, and destroy. This is why Paul strongly states:

> *2 Corinthians 10:3–5 (NAS): For though we walk in the flesh, we do not war according to the flesh,*
>
> *4 for the weapons of our warfare are not of the flesh, but divinely powerful for the destruction of fortresses.*
>
> *5 We are destroying speculations and every lofty thing raised up against the knowledge of God, and <u>we are taking every thought captive to the obedience of Christ,</u>*

Interesting that Paul talks about this process in the context of warfare. Kings must master the language of Heaven in order to be keenly aware of WHO is speaking in the forum of their minds at all times so that they can take unholy, disobedient thoughts captive and reject their influence as an act of spiritual war. When we get good at this, we can succeed at tearing down speculations and lofty things raised up against the knowledge of God.

So how do we know who is speaking?

This isn't formulaic, but I believe there are universal principles that guide how the King of Kings communicates with his sons. The first principle that has been most helpful to me is that the voice of God will always carry the timbre and qualities of the fruits of HIS Holy Spirit. In short, His voice sounds like love, joy, peace, patience, kindness, goodness, faithfulness, gentleness, and self-control. But this is not an exhaustive list. I've also heard Him speak with power, confidence, wisdom, humor, and ease.

Often He doesn't speak with words at all, but more with a sense of knowing in my "gut". Sometimes Holy Spirit will speak through a picture in my mind's eye. They often come at weird times and are in sharp contrast to what I'm feeling or thinking at the moment. We often use colloquialisms like "that thought sure came out of left field" or "that wasn't even on my radar" to describe events like these. The point is that they don't flow with the natural thoughts you're having at that moment. They are disruptive or counterintuitive.

One key for me to identify these words as Holy Spirit is that His words sound better than what I could think up on my own. They're kinder, more powerful thoughts than my natural mind is contemplating at that moment. Perhaps in a desperate situation you think of something that fills you with hope, or get a great idea about how to solve a problem that you could not figure out. Perhaps you have a kind thought about a person who's wounded you. I've learned that this is almost always the voice of the Holy Spirit speaking to me, not my internal voice, and not the voice of my enemy.

In Isaiah, we learn the following about Jesus.

> *Isaiah 9:6–7 (NLT): For a child is born to us,*
>
> *a son is given to us.*
>
> *The government will rest on his shoulders.*
>
> *And he will be called:*
>
> *Wonderful Counselor, Mighty God,*
>
> *Everlasting Father, Prince of Peace.*
>
> *7 His government and its peace*
>
> *will never end.*

I'm learning that based on Jesus' identity and the names He's been given, I can expect Him to speak a certain way. As the Wonderful Counselor, I expect Him to be wise and provide incredible revelation about whatever I'm going through. As Mighty God, I expect His strength and incredible confidence to come through in His words. As my Prince of Peace, I would never expect His voice to sound anxious or filled with uncertainty, but instead calm and reassuring to my spirit and mind. In addition, we have the four gospels which provide us firsthand accounts and recordings of the Jesus' own words. In these texts, we can detect His tone and personality as He interacted with [illegible]ples, demons, Pharisees, sinners, and the world around Him. [illegible]ve believe in the triune God - Father, Son, and Holy Spirit - [illegible] that there is a common expression of their "voice" for us to h[illegible]dentify. Again, is it any wonder that Jesus confidently states t[illegible]eep would know His voice?

[illegible] detecting the specific voice of Holy Spirit, I've also learned to [illegible]e my voice. My voice isn't "random" either. Because of my personality, my thoughts fit into a pretty linear pattern. I think "I'm hungry" and then my next thought is about food, what I'd prefer at that moment, where to find it, how much work it's going to take to prepare it, whether it's worth it - you get the idea.

"Random" thoughts that interrupt my thoughts like little lightning strikes in my mind are often the Holy Spirit - IF they follow the rules above about how they "sound". Holy Spirit is good at interrupting my thoughts and I'm getting better at detecting His voice in my Spirit, and allowing it to come up into my conscious thoughts instead of brushing it aside.

The point is that kings must learn how NOT to plow blindly through our day governed by our natural brain and its simple intellectual process. We must learn to hear and speak the language of Heaven and let it govern our life.

I can't tell you the number of times I've received calls from friends during tough times and the story almost always starts the same. They "randomly" thought about me and felt prompted to reach out and see how I was doing. Often those calls have been timely and gave me hope to get through a hard situation.

You may have been conditioned your whole life to think your thoughts are just the random collision of atoms, neurons, and hormones bubbling and bouncing around in your brain. It's not true. You're a spiritual being, not just a brain. Don't misunderstand, your brain is magnificent! It's helpful for solving problems, doing math, keeping your heart beating, directing your body to repair itself, and thousands of voluntary and involuntary functions we're continuing to discover even to this present day. But reality is that your brain will go in a box when you die. Your spirit will live on forever and as our scripture above states, God has instructed His kings to lean NOT on their own understanding (brain) but to acknowledge Him in all their ways. My interpretation of this verse: Holy Spirit is in the room with you at all times and He's in charge. Acknowledge this and submit all your ways - the way you parent, the way you work, the way you make decisions, the way you love your spouse - to His instruction and He will empower you to live in flow, providing you spiritual wisdom to execute plans and direct your life.

So what does the enemy's voice sound like? Great question. For starters, they sound like the opposite of the fruit of the spirit. This may not sound all that profound, but when you really understand how restricted Satan and his demons are, it will become a key to detecting him every time. Remember, he's been DIS-empowered and stripped of his authority by Jesus. He's impotent. Even his "ace in the hole", death itself, has no power over us any longer. But he is cunning, and he knows he can only influence us if we GIVE him influence. Therefore, he uses deception as a subtle entry point, a foothold, of influence.

But he's limited. He's the father of lies, so he can't tell the truth - at least not the whole truth - as we see in the temptation of Jesus in the wilderness. So your first clue: if something is factually inaccurate, then it was probably spoken by him.

Moreover, he's been kicked out of heaven, removed from the presence of God, and has no access to peace, love, joy, creativity, patience, goodness, kindness, etc. He now lives an agonizing and psychotic existence on Earth, locked into time and space, far removed from the unlimited resources of heaven, waiting for his impending judgment and ultimate destruction. So clue number two: his "voice" often sounds angry, depressed, anxious, fearful, and filled with pain. Even when it is masked in logic, or peace, you can detect the thin facade covering up the intense malevolence he has for us. If our spiritual defenses are down and we don't detect him as the source, or we entertain his thoughts, then we'll ALWAYS be tempted to do something compromising, dangerous, hurtful, or destructive. The Bible calls him the "Accuser" and so his voice sounds like shame and accusation. He speaks through fearful thoughts, constant "what if" thoughts, predetermined negative outcomes, and panic. Clue number three: the pace of the thoughts is fast and furious. One of his strategies is to bombard your mind with rapid-fire thoughts to create chaos and to get your mind spinning out of control in confusion. He loves it when he can get you worked up into a mental frenzy with no answers, solutions, or hope. Remember, his intent is to steal, kill, and destroy - John 10:10.

SUBMIT ALL YOUR WAYS - THE WAY YOU PARENT, THE WAY YOU WORK, THE WAY YOU MAKE DECISIONS, THE WAY YOU LOVE YOUR SPOUSE - TO HIS INSTRUCTION AND HOLY SPIRIT WILL EMPOWER YOU TO LIVE IN FLOW, PROVIDING YOU SPIRITUAL WISDOM TO EXECUTE PLANS AND DIRECT YOUR LIFE.

One challenge in detecting him is the fact that he has successfully gained control over the language of our culture and his "voice" is the dominant voice you hear in most of our news, media, and entertainment. It's so common that we've become desensitized to it and we've normalized his rhetoric to such a degree that we can easily come under his influence without realizing it. However, if we know Jesus' voice, the contrast between the voice of our loving Saviour and our mortal enemy couldn't be more distinct, and the forum discussions in our mind become much simpler to navigate.

To master the spiritual language of heaven, I've found it helpful to practice silence and actively listen for His voice. The spirit of religion has, again, attempted to sabotage this ancient practice by turning it into a Christian daily task we can quickly check off. We often refer to it as "quiet time" or "daily devotions" and we've altered the practice of patiently listening to him, and meditating on His words. It has become a quick 5 minute pit stop in our day where we consume information about Him. While this isn't wrong, it is definitely not complete. This can become another subtle and elegant trap laid by our enemy. I mean, who could argue that reading about God is a bad thing? No one. Because it's not a bad thing. But it's not the same as connecting with the PERSON of Holy Spirit. Don't believe me, consider this analogy: reading about sex is a completely different experience that actual intimacy with my wife. Forgive the extreme example, but if we're to step into our role as kings, we need to understand the stark contrast between knowledge and experience. It may also help you to know that this level of intimacy is used in the Bible to describe our relationship to Jesus himself. We are identified as the bride of Christ. Don't get hung up on the analogy. The point is that good kings have experience, not theories. One of my pastors and mentors used to teach about an ancient practice called lectio divina. It is a beautifully slow way to examine scripture where we allow Holy Spirit to lead the process, highlight passages, and provide insight as we sit with Him and meditate on the word together in relationship.

This subtle shift away from experiencing something firsthand through relationship and toward consuming information about something has sabotaged an entire generation in our culture. We have young people who know the top 10 best places to visit in the world not because they've been there to experience it, but because they can Google it. I'd like to suggest that this is largely the result of an educational system that accepts knowledge as the equivalent to experience. Therefore, we have business classes taught by teachers who've never owned a business, home economics and health classes taught by people who've never run a household or had children, and PE taught by people who may not even take care of their own bodies - and we accept this as normal. We should be utterly offended by the spirit behind this because its intent is to confuse us to where we cannot distinguish a counterfeit thing from the authentic thing. It's not a simple oversight or blind spot in the educational system, it's a spiritual attack on humanity designed to condition the human mind to blindly accept lies from hell as equivalent to revelation from Heaven.

Believers are not immune to these phenomena because our "education" about spiritual things occurs within the same basic academic context and structure as I described above. I have to admit that looking back, I find it astonishing that I sat through several college religion courses taught by an atheist religion professor who, ironically, was head of the religion department of my Christian college - and this was considered perfectly acceptable. It's this mindset that allows smart people to adopt ridiculous intellectual positions. And it's what has produced an entire Western Church that believes that knowing ABOUT Jesus is the same as knowing Him. Indeed, this religion professor knew lots of facts about Jesus, but had no revelation of the Holy Spirit's power in his own life. Similarly, we can go to church and listen to worship music ABOUT Jesus, we hear preachers teach ABOUT Jesus, we listen to Christian radio stations that play songs ABOUT Jesus, we read books ABOUT Jesus. We can study Him like an abstract concept. We research the intricate meaning of Greek words to comprehend the historical context and meaning of the Bible to better understand what He SAID in the past. And we can convince ourselves that this is the sum total of what it means to be a Christ follower. I admit that in my spiritual journey, I've likely spent 10x more time engaged in educating myself than sitting, seeking, and listening to hear Him speak fresh words of life to me. Is it any wonder why I've struggled to gain victory over my giants and have felt alone when facing trials, problems or challenges in life. Is it really a mystery why we wrestle with feelings of abandonment when storms of life broadside us? Is it not obvious why the Western world has essentially concluded that religion doesn't work and people are leaving churches in droves?

If I, as a believer, can't make religion "work", then how much less the non-believer who is looking for answers. If I carry disillusionment and disappointment about God around like relational baggage from a failed marriage and go to coping mechanisms to get by, then what can I offer the non-believer? If I struggle with hidden sin, guilt, shame, under the weight of a performance-based system that produces anything EXCEPT freedom, then how can I carry out my assignment to set captives free? If I feel abandoned by God and can't hear His voice, then how do I offer hope to anyone else?

If this sounds familiar, may I gently suggest that you may need to put down the books (yes, even this book!), and get connected to the PERSON of Holy Spirit. Kings must learn to silence their brains and cultivate an inner place of peace and rest where the voice of the Holy Spirit can be heard. Kings, you already know that counterfeits are everywhere, but they won't help you when life blows up. Counterfeits come in many appealing packages. Perhaps you fell in love with a concept and a theory about God, or a friendly group of really nice people, or got swept away in an emotional high from a wow experience in worship. I love all these things, and none of them are inherently wrong, but without a personal connection with Holy Spirit, it's not faith. It's just like any other club, hobby, or interest around which people will gather.

Many people enter the Kingdom with an intimate experience with God. They hear His voice in a moment of need; they experience a miracle, deliverance, healing; something relational, tangible, and real, where Holy Spirit "introduces" Himself to the individual. However, if not mentored by a spiritual father who can teach them how to abide IN Christ, a religious spirit will hijack the experience and shift them to an intellectually oriented, self-improvement "gospel". Inside this framework, information acquisition and good behavior become the highest goal, while relational connection through experiences with Holy Spirit are viewed with caution and suspicion as the enemy attempts to snuff out the fire of our faith.

So how do we recalibrate?

STEP 1 | Our Proverbs passage teaches us to not lean on our own understanding. Instead, we acknowledge Holy Spirit is in the room with you and He's in charge.

STEP 2 | Talk to Him about what you're going through. Ask Him specific questions and listen for His voice. Learn to detect the "sound" of His voice. As we've discussed, He speaks in thoughts and pictures that pop into your mind, feelings in your gut, scripture, or the voice of trustworthy, Spirit-filled friends in your community. Become a student of the sound of His voice, as distinct from yours, and the enemy's. Enjoy the forum discussion in your mind where He will meet you and offer you grace, peace, and extraordinary insight. Don't judge yourself harshly if you don't "hear" anything at first or have trouble distinguishing who is "speaking". Give yourself grace and stay engaged. It's a process.

STEP 3 | Stop letting your brain and your enemies filibuster the forum in your mind as you meditate. Practice self-control over your thoughts and take captive and reject any thoughts that seek to disturb your peace or crowd out Holy Spirit's influence and voice. Speak out loud to bind the enemy's voice and silence him repeatedly, if necessary. Take action. Your mind is a battleground and don't assume he's going to give up the territory he's taken over without a fight. But this is a fight you CAN win.

2 Timothy 1:7 (AMP): 7 For God did not give us a spirit of timidity (of cowardice, of craven and cringing and fawning fear), but [He has given us a spirit] of power and of love and of calm and well-balanced mind and discipline and self-control.

STEP 4 | When you start to feel negative emotions - fear, stress, chaos, etc. stop what you're doing - physically stop - don't grab a coping mechanism - don't distract yourself with busyness. Listen for His voice to speak to you. He will speak. Circumstances may not immediately resolve, but allow yourself to be encouraged by Jesus' words in Matthew as He silences the enemy's voice.

Matthew 4:4 (NLT): People do not live by bread alone, but by every word that comes from the mouth of God.

So listen to the words that come from HIS mouth if you want to LIVE. As you invest in this process, a reassuring hope will rise in your spirit, as a lightness in your emotions, and peace that passes understanding shift from intellectual theory to reality. That's what connecting with Him feels like, a river of life, a flow.

STEP 5 | After He speaks, celebrate. Indulge yourself - have a drink, a meal, tell a fellow king, go do something you like! Celebrate the fact that you were able to connect with the God of the universe in a real way. Celebrate your victory,

> that you've regained control over your thoughts and taken territory back from the enemy. This is no small thing and you can be sure that your Father in Heaven is excited to celebrate you in your success.

One of my favorite sayings I hear my friend IBen say is this, "When the battle heats up, I check my heart." Indeed. Whether we're simply starting our work day or facing serious challenges, we need to deliberately take inventory of our mind, body, and spirit to make sure we're functioning from a place of flow. I love working with IBen because while he is a talented online marketer, a genius content developer, and a sage king filled with wisdom, he understands that his first identity is a king, surrendered to the King of Kings. For this reason, most of our meetings begin with worship because he wants to make sure that we acknowledge Holy Spirit is in the room and he wants to thank Him for loving us and for helping us with every detail of the tasks at hand. I can't tell you how many times we've taken a two-hour meeting and spent the first hour worshipping, singing, and praying to align our hearts and minds FIRMLY with Holy Spirit in flow. From this place, it's common for us to get 3-4 hours' worth of work done in the remaining hour. We're always amazed at how gracious Holy Spirit is to accelerate our thought processes and provide wisdom to execute the tasks at hand with supernatural speed and excellence. We are discovering that Proverbs 3: 5-6 is significantly more practical than we realized!

Kings, you know what to do. I pray you are released from striving and the bondage of intellectualism. I bless you with a new capacity, and an ever-increasing ability to hear and experience Holy Spirit's "voice" through your new native tongue, the language of Heaven, and to invite Him and His supernatural abilities into every area of your life so you can function from a place of ease and flow.

Chapter 14

TO HEAL OR NOT TO HEAL… IS THAT THE QUESTION?

I grew up in a Christian home where church and faith were a central part of our life and community. While my parents and the church I grew up in did a wonderful job emphasizing the importance of Scripture and building a solid foundation of Biblical truth for my life, I don't recall learning much about the Holy Spirit. Though, to be fair, our church had a prayer chain and I can remember how faithfully my mother would take down prayer requests and then diligently call the next several people in her network to ask them to pray. I wish I could go back and glean testimonies from those days because, in retrospect, I'm sure that Holy Spirit moved mightily through the faithful prayers of the saints in that little country church we attended.

I also recall testimonies like when my mother felt the presence of Holy Spirit wrap around her in a protective, peace-filled shield as she knelt under the kitchen table, holding my infant sister in her arms while a tornado destroyed the old farmhouse we lived in. She and my sister emerged without a scratch. I recall my father's testimony of having his wallet returned to him just days before he and I were going to attend a Promise Keepers' event. He had lost the wallet a few days earlier, which was filled with cash in preparation for our trip. We felt that the loss was an attack designed by the enemy to discourage us from attending the event, but as we prayed, we felt compelled to go anyway - with or without the wallet and the money. Upon making that decision, the phone rang, and a fellow truck driver on the other end of the line shared that he'd found the wallet, seen the CDL license, and felt compelled to contact the owner and return it. Not a single dollar was missing, and we had the wallet back before we left on the trip. It was a testimony that encouraged the entire group of men from our church that would attend the Promise Keepers' event, and it was a testimony of God redeeming and restoring what the enemy had stolen.

I can vividly remember having encounters with God, and even demons, that I didn't really understand or have language for at the time. As a child I could hear Holy Spirit speak clearly and kindly to me as I would pray simple prayers. However, over time, I unknowingly drifted into intellectualism, duped by an imposter religious spirit that encouraged me to put away "childish" ideas about a supernatural relationship with the Spirit of God. I developed a hard heart toward people and traditions that "moved in the Spirit" and became suspicious of so-called "manifestations of the Spirit". This religious spirit warned me, ironically, through misapplied scripture, that the Devil comes "masquerading as an angel of light". This deceptive spirit taught me to idolize intellectualism, and I learned to argue to defend my tradition's theological positions and how to debunk the theologies of other "lesser" traditions and "isms". It stole my innocent, child-like faith that believed in an enormous God, and a small devil, and instead groomed me to be a great Pharisee that saw a huge devil and a small, ineffective God that needed my help to persuade people to join His Kingdom through superior intellectual arguments rather than manifestations of His power and goodness. Sadly, I didn't even know it was happening until my supernatural deliverance encounter rocked my intellectual world.

An unintended consequence of this demonic influence was a dismissal of the power of prayer and the Holy Spirit's involvement in and influence over my first-realm experiences. So, on the rare occasion that I prayed for people to be healed, I hardly gave any thought to what might be happening simultaneously in the unseen realm. Honestly, I saw little to no consistent correlation between my prayers and the results, which left me unmotivated to pray and caused me to adopt a broken perspective on the power of prayer and a worse perspective on the sovereignty of God.

In college, I took part in InterVarsity, a college ministry and missions organization. In our large group meetings, we discovered the power of worship and its ability to usher in the presence of Holy Spirit. At the same time, a local Reformed church in our city broke out in revival through the power of Holy Spirit experienced in worship. Both on campus and at the local church, the services were filled with an indescribable energy and joy like I'd never really felt in a corporate service before. People would run into the building to get seats when the doors would open. Our campus ministry ballooned to over 600 people on a campus of only 1200 students, and the local church service called the "7:10 Service" drew people from hours away every Sunday evening. It was as if Holy Spirit was stirring the waters for revival as He introduced us to a new facet of His glory. We hosted conferences on hearing the voice of God, worship, and healing, and I attended nearly every class and conference I could.

For the first time in my life, the supernatural stories I read in the Scriptures transitioned from theories to first-hand experiences. They took on new meaning as we saw deliverances and healings break out here and there. After college, our church cast a vision for planting additional "Word and Spirit" churches and I was asked to help lead worship at one of the satellite campuses in a neighboring town about one year into the plant. It was during this assignment that my hunger and reverence for Holy Spirit was truly solidified. It was normal in worship to feel the presence so strong I couldn't hardly continue to sing. I spent the better portion of a decade serving there. During that time, I experienced healing, and we saw people with stage-four cancer healed and given extended life. We even had a member of our church raised from the dead through the power of corporate prayer. We saw tons of people freed from drug and alcohol addiction, delivered from demonic oppression, and give their lives to Christ. At one point, we were visited by a group of ministry school students from Redding, CA. Through their ministry, we continued to discover amazing new elements of our inheritance in the Kingdom. We saw legs grow out, chronic pain healed, and experienced the power of prophetic encouragement. Today I am privileged to take part in a new assignment with a vibrant faith community in Redding, CA, where God continues to snowball my understanding of His Spirit. I'm discovering His outrageous goodness, even in trials, as He reveals new facets of His infinite Kingdom. We continue to learn from spiritual fathers and friends, new and old, and the Kingdom, and our King, just keeps getting bigger, and better.

However, not every prayer we've prayed has been answered, at least not in the way we wanted. Some of our friends have gone home to be with Jesus, despite our fervent prayers for healing. Some of our dearest friends and family have experienced devastating, life-altering losses and setbacks. And we have personally experienced our own difficult circumstances, including job loss, financial challenges, relational and mental breakdowns, illnesses, and much more. In these moments, I'm reminded that the battle is incredibly real and I'm so humbled by the strength and courage I see in people who persevere through the pain.

As I've sought understanding of this through scripture and from Holy Spirit, I'm learning that God's ongoing and unwavering promise is to use ALL situations for good for His sons and daughters. As we learn in Romans 8:28, He will ALWAYS do that, whether or not the circumstances resolve according to my expectations.

> *Romans 8:28–29 (NLT): And we know God causes everything to work together for the good of those who love God and are called according to his purpose for them. 29 For God knew his people in advance, and he chose them to become like his Son, so that his Son would be the firstborn among many brothers and sisters.*

The reality of Christ crucified and resurrected means that sickness, disease, poverty, lack, blindness, mental illness, depression, anxiety, and all other forms of spiritual, mental, and physical bondage and affliction have been subjugated to the authority of the resurrected God-man, our brother, Jesus. That means He can undo all the evil works of the Devil at any moment, and indeed He will return to do just that one glorious day in the future. However, He's chosen to refrain from direct judgment of Satan and his works for this current epoch season, the Church age, and chosen instead to empower His followers to do His work to set captives free as ambassadors of His Kingdom. Jesus is our model and His explicit instructions are for us to be like Him.

Obviously, in this broken first realm, evil afflictions manifest and affect our lives. In this context, as He did in so many other epoch seasons throughout Scripture, God can, and will, flip these evil works around to heal and renew people for His glory. I have seen this time and time again. I don't believe He inflicts illness, loss, and pain on His children to teach them a lesson. I believe Jesus died to deliver us from these things, and His atoning sacrifice has removed the stain of sin that would warrant punishment. However, I would suggest that few things can tenderize our hearts and bring us to a merciful point of surrender to the King and His Kingdom like pain. I'd also suggest that it's difficult to become a giant-killer with no giants in the land and there is incredible value in the war we wage to take them out. In the heat of battle is where I often experience Him most as He sets the stage for a miraculous victory or shows me His profound love and awesome power. Battles also reveal my own blind spots or weaknesses and in that weakness I discover His strength, and a new place of authority and strength. The complex nature of God is such that He's always doing multiple things in our hearts through every situation we face and He is intentional to work EVERYTHING for your good as one of His beloved sons. As Romans 8:28 promises, all these things will ultimately work together for good because it is His divine merciful purpose to save and bless us, who are called according to His purposes. I also love verse 29, which identifies us as His people, and His sons, and the brothers of Jesus. In short, if you're in the family, then your right and privilege is to witness your Father work every situation in your life for good, in the end, regardless of the pain or trauma that you may experience in the moment.

Kings, let's talk about rebellion for just a moment. As I stated, I do not believe that God causes pain under the new covenant in Jesus' blood. But I'd humbly suggest that we experience self-inflicted pain because of rebellion in our heart, or sin in our lives, and we reap the harvest that we've sown. In these moments, I believe Romans 8:28-29 has particular power and relevance because we know that even in the midst of our own mess; He is STILL working all things for our good. Wow... what a kind and gracious King of Kings we serve. I believe that in these moments, like a loving father, He will step aside and allow a measure of the pain and suffering we've sown to be reaped in our life to reveal parts of our own heart that need to be surrendered. My friend Mark describes it like this. God can, and sometimes will, in essence, fling you around the dark side of the moon, giving you over to its gravitational pull, to where you're isolated and out of control. These "prodigal son" seasons of darkness are often where the greatest spiritual hunger and growth occur. When we emerge from the darkness, He's there, with open arms ready to receive us, and at those moments we're truly, genuinely ready to receive Him. It is in these moments that bumper sticker faith transitions from a slogan to a very personal, real, faith.

He's not threatened by the process and not insecure about the outcome and, because we have this Romans 8:28 promise, we don't have to be either. Jesus turned the tables on sorrow, sickness, loss, sin, even death. These all now work in unison for our good and serve His ultimate purposes to empower His kings to step into victory.

So is death, disease, or affliction ever from God? Never from God? Sometimes from God? Much smarter people than I have debated this for centuries and honestly, I don't care to get caught in these theological weeds. I see from Scripture that Jesus himself raised people from the dead who had been the victim of an evil attack that caused their untimely death. He did this to fulfill His Isaiah 61 manifesto, which He made known at the start of His earthly ministry, and to establish the supremacy of His Heavenly Kingdom over everything on Earth, even death. He also instructed His followers that they should do the same when He sent them out saying:

> *Matthew 10:7–8 (NAS): And as you go, preach, saying, 'The kingdom of heaven is at hand.'*
>
> *8 "Heal the sick, raise the dead, cleanse the lepers, cast out demons. Freely you received, freely give.*

So clearly, death is not always *from* God. It may be an opportunity for Holy Spirit to use us to broker a miracle from Heaven to demonstrate Jesus' power and to advance His Kingdom.

I believe A king's first responsibility when faced with difficult situations is not to slap some rote theological formula onto the situation and pretend to have the "answer" because we read a book about it. Rather it is the precise moment we earnestly seek Holy Spirit to discern His will and humbly align with His life-giving plan for each unique person and circumstance. It is not helpful or spiritual to offer vain, powerless prayers and to hide behind God's sovereignty as an excuse for our ineffectiveness. But it's equally unholy to whip ourselves into a spiritual frenzy, to manipulate God into performing a miracle, like the prophets of Baal. Kings humbly fall in line with Holy

Spirit, yield to His plan, and pray bold prayers that unlock His power to accomplish His will - with no other agenda. As we embrace intimacy with Holy Spirit as our starting place, He will provide us incredible wisdom to navigate these delicate moments and walk with His precious people in their pain. Remember, for God SO LOVED the world... Kings, your assignment is not necessarily to come up with the right answer according to Calvinist or Arminian theology. Your assignment is to bring dead things to life, whether that means literally raising a dead person, or speaking life over a broken-hearted survivor - we are free to let Holy Spirit inform us and empower us for the assignment.

I BELIEVE A KING'S FIRST RESPONSIBILITY WHEN FACED WITH DIFFICULT SITUATIONS IS NOT TO SLAP SOME ROTE THEOLOGICAL FORMULA ONTO THE SITUATION AND PRETEND TO HAVE THE "ANSWER" BECAUSE WE READ A BOOK ABOUT IT.

Chapter 15

KINGS ARE STUDENTS OF MOMENTS: *THE TONGUE*

Kings are students of moments. For example, the moment when a problem hits and you shift from faith filled optimism into frustration, fear or doubt. That's a pretty significant moment. How about the moment when your spouse says something harmless, but the enemy triggers you by converting their harmless statement into something malicious and hurtful, at which point you lash out in retaliation? Whew... that's a REALLY important moment.

Our ability to navigate these very familiar moments can mean the difference between functioning in our rightful place of grace and power or devolving into a frustrated and self-destructive victim. Kings, this is a big deal. When we entertain negative thoughts for over 30-60 seconds, then the surrounding atmosphere can begin to shift toward negativity as our words become critical, judgmental, and we align with our spiritual adversaries. If I don't apprehend this moment, then a cloud of gloom and despair hovers over me and those I lead. Worse yet, I lose access to the creativity required to solve the problem and navigate the situation as I voluntarily shift my perspective away from the Heavenly realm and my King - who has all the answers.

This has devastating implications for those I lead, beginning with myself, and extending to my family, church, business, workplace and any other place I've been granted influence and authority by our King. Negativity is a spiritual killer! Before you think I've set an unattainable standard of perpetual positivity, let me be clear. God knew this would be a challenge for us as kings and has given us a handy tool called repentance to get our minds unstuck and back on track when we don't navigate these moments/attacks well. And should we hurt people around us during a momentary lapse, we have another tool to help us clean up the mess, asking forgiveness from those we've hurt.

These two tools are a regular part of a king's personal spiritual arsenal. Just like a dagger and a sword on his belt, repentance and forgiveness are two close-combat spiritual weapons that we need to put on every morning, just like putting on socks and underwear. Without them, you're not equipped to handle the challenges of your day and probably not going to lead well.

Getting good at navigating this moment looks like repenting and asking forgiveness quickly. In the past, I could stay frustrated and stuck for days and weeks. And I'm sad to report that even after I got my mind "right" and regained perspective, it would often be days before I would seek those I'd wounded to seek their forgiveness - if I did it at all.

As a king, I'm responsible for the culture of my home, my church, my workplace, my kingdom and neglecting the responsibility to repent and ask forgiveness produces a closed-off culture where transparent and truthful communication is unsafe. In this culture, people won't be honest for fear that they'll be criticized and shamed for their poor performance or mistakes. In this culture, people function in fear and avoid confrontation, especially with the king.

I used to create this culture around me and it eventually became apparent to me in the way my wife and children hid mistakes from me, instead of coming to me with their problems. It was a sobering day when I realized the anti-Christ culture I had created. It was the product of many moments where I'd chosen to align my heart with criticism and judgment rather than kindness and grace.

However, through the Holy Spirit's patient teaching, I've learned how to use repentance and forgiveness, first with myself, then with my family, and then with others I lead, to shift to a culture of connection, safety, and creativity. In His wisdom, Holy Spirit has made this one so simple to understand and execute. We can choose the culture of Earth filled with judgment, performance, criticism, and hiding; or the culture of Heaven, filled with purpose, forgiveness, grace, and blessing. When the enemy lures us into the Earthly culture, repentance and forgiveness are the tools that get us free and reconnected to Heaven and the reconnection can happen in a moment.

Moments of mis-alignment can be hard to detect if we're distracted, not self-aware, or emotionally disconnected. But they are important because when we shift into unbelief, fear, or anger, then we effectively abandon our post as ambassadors of the King of Kings and His Kingdom. While our citizenship is never in question, our connection to Heaven's supply lines and resources can be temporarily severed, leaving us, those we lead, and our territory vulnerable. As any military veteran will tell you, that's no joke. These moments are important. For your sake and the sake of the people around you these moments are everything. Kings know this and exercise self-control. More importantly, they are ruthless with the thoughts they entertain. They are relentless about

WE CAN CHOOSE THE CULTURE OF EARTH FILLED WITH JUDGMENT, PERFORMANCE, CRITICISM, AND HIDING; OR THE CULTURE OF HEAVEN, FILLED WITH PURPOSE, FORGIVENESS, GRACE, AND BLESSING.

guarding their heart and mind. Scripture teaches us that out of the overflow of heart, the mouth speaks. Kings recognize that the harsh criticism or judgment they entertain in their mind could come out of their mouth with potentially devastating consequences if the internal "filter" temporarily malfunctions. Do you know one of the most distinct characteristics of a king? They don't really need an internal filter, because their hearts are pure. Notice I didn't say they were perfect people. I said their hearts were pure. If your heart is pure, then what comes out doesn't require a filter. James has some pretty strong things to say about our tongues.

> *James 3:1–12 (NLT): Dear brothers and sisters, not many of you should become teachers in the church, for we who teach will be judged more strictly. 2 Indeed, we all make many mistakes. For if we could control our tongues, we would be perfect and could also control ourselves in every other way.*
>
> *3 We can make a large horse go wherever we want by means of a small bit in its mouth. 4 And a small rudder makes a huge ship turn wherever the pilot chooses to go, even though the winds are strong. 5 In the same way, the tongue is a small thing that makes grand speeches.*
>
> *But a tiny spark can set a great forest on fire. 6 And among all the parts of the body, the tongue is a flame of fire. It is a whole world of wickedness corrupting your entire body. It can set your whole life on fire, for it is set on fire by hell itself.*
>
> *7 People can tame all kinds of animals, birds, reptiles, and fish, 8 but no one can tame the tongue. It is restless and evil, full of deadly poison. 9 Sometimes it praises our Lord and Father, and sometimes it curses those who have been made in the image of God. 10 And so blessing and cursing come pouring out of the same mouth. Surely, my brothers and sisters, this is not right! 11 Does a spring of water bubble out with both fresh water and bitter water? 12 Does a fig tree produce olives, or a grapevine produce figs? No, and you can't draw fresh water from a salty spring.*

Our words reveal what is on the inside, and if we are internally misaligned with Heaven, it can be ugly. A hallmark of immaturity is the impulse to speak too quickly, or to lose control of your emotions, your thoughts, and then your tongue. Sadly, I functioned this way for many years and damaged my marriage and my relationships with my children, loved ones, and friends. The collateral damage has been significant. But repentance and forgiveness are a spiritual balm that has healed, and continues to heal, many wounds.

Kings, this is so important because the way you speak brings about life or death. As the King's ambassador, your role in the Earth is to proclaim the GOOD news of Jesus Christ, His victory over evil and the wonders of His Kingdom. You are not to join in the chorus of complaining, judgment, and criticism so common throughout the Earth. It's really simple, and also really impossible to do this well apart from the power of the Holy Spirit.

I've discovered that for me, the impulse to be critical resulted from my own self-criticism. Kings, this is important because there is no power to offer grace to others until you give grace to yourself. As we've said over and over, God, your Heavenly Father and your King, has resolved in His own heart to never leave or forsake you. He's not angry or critical toward you and He's not tracking your bad behavior or failures. It's the ultimate insult to Him, and a worse insult to His son, for you to hold yourself to some unrealistic standard and be harsh or critical of yourself. The very notion that you're still under the law of performance is a lie from the pit of hell. Reject the lie, take back your identity from the enemy, and reclaim your honor as a forgiven son. Step back into your post. You're a foreign ambassador from a superior Kingdom filled with grace and kindness. Refugees and orphans from this world are streaming in and it's your duty to welcome them as the King wishes. We can't afford to get swept away in criticism and judgment or shame and despair because we lose focus in weak moments. The world needs you to become a master at detecting your enemy's tactics in these moments, to quickly repent, get back your focus, clean up your mess by asking forgiveness if necessary, and continue on as King's royal ambassador.

> *Proverbs 4:23–25 (NAS): Watch over your heart with all diligence,*
> *For from it flow the springs of life.*
> *24 Put away from you a deceitful mouth*
> *And put devious speech far from you.*
> *25 Let your eyes look directly ahead*
> *And let your gaze be fixed straight in front of you.*

Chapter 16

THE HOLY SPIRIT IN THE SEX STORE

I grew up on a Midwest farm in a very entrepreneurial family, so we raised corn, soybeans, livestock, and my father also owned a small metal fabrication and manufacturing company and a trucking company. Among many things, he always loved driving, and I inherited the same love. It doesn't really matter what I'm driving; I love it. Motorcycles, go-karts, semi-trucks, tractors, ATVs, UTVs, I love them all. When I was young, I wanted to be a race car driver and my walls were covered with exotic car posters and monster trucks. And while I have had the chance to own and drive some fabulous cars, it is still on my bucket list to drive a monster jam truck before I die!

Interstate 44 across Oklahoma is a wonderfully uneventful stretch of road connecting Oklahoma City in the center of the state to Tulsa in the East. It was a hot summer afternoon in July 2013 and I'd already been driving for several hours en route to my next sales meeting. I was co-owner and Vice President of Sales for a chemical manufacturing company that made foam insulation, epoxy flooring, roof coatings and a variety of other construction products. I had a team of salespeople who covered the United States for our company, but I always liked to remain connected to key customers and was always up for a road trip. Typically, I would bring my family on trips like these and we'd work in some sightseeing and family fun along the way, but this was a quick trip and I was solo.

On solo trips with extended windshield time, it was normal for me to put on a good podcast of my favorite preacher or listen to worship music, talk radio, or sometimes just drive in silence and connect with Holy Spirit for hours and I loved it.

It was about 3 pm and I was cruising at about 90 mph in the worship "zone" (where the speed limits are higher - everyone knows this), when I passed a sign for an adult sex store a few miles ahead. As was always the case, I thought nothing of it and went right back to worshipping. A few miles later I passed it, a completely dilapidated building on the left side of the road with an old sign out front that advertised toys, novelties, DVD's, etc. Suddenly my heart started racing and I felt this urge to stop at this store. I suppressed this urge, rebuked the spirit of lust, and like a good Christian, I sped past the exit, leaving the building in my rearview.

I had struggled with pornography off and on since I was a teenager and while I'd never actually been inside an adult store; I knew that my own battles with lust and pornography were real. By God's mercy and some powerful prayers from my wife, I'd been delivered from addiction to porn and I knew how devastating it could be for me to go into a place like that and potentially "fall off the wagon". I wanted nothing to do with that.

For 15 miles I rebuked the spirit of lust, resisted temptation, bound the devil, loosed peace, declared purity over my mind... and nothing worked. I prayed in tongues; I prayed in English, I laughed, I worshipped, I sat in silence; I tried a couple of different podcasts. My heart just kept pounding louder and louder. My palms began to sweat. I had no idea what was happening. Was this some next-level attack from some demonic "general" or what?

Strangely, the impulse to stop didn't feel sensual or sexual at all. It was just a weird gut-level urging to stop. Eventually, I had this completely ridiculous thought. What if it's the Holy Spirit? No. Couldn't be. Not possible. Holy Spirit doesn't lead us into temptation, He delivers us FROM it. Nope. Nope. Nope. Not gonna do it. But the thought wouldn't go away and finally I asked a ridiculous question that up till this moment had been unthinkable, "Holy Spirit, is this you?"

A resounding YES dropped into my gut. I pulled over to the side of the road, and sat for a few minutes, sweaty, heart pounding, not sure what to do. I honestly thought I was being deceived by some spirit of deception who was counterfeiting the Holy Spirit's voice, but how could that be??? Finally, in disgust, I slammed on the gas and sped to the next exit about ½ a mile ahead. Not sure why, but I started driving like a maniac. Perhaps I was hoping the long arm of the law would pull me over before I got back there and I wouldn't have to go through with whatever "assignment" this was.

For 15 minutes I drove back down interstate 44, fuming mad, arguing with Holy Spirit about how out of bounds it was to go into an adult sex novelties store. My mind was so closed off that I couldn't think of a single good thing that could come of this. I have a very transparent relationship with my wife and I could just imagine walking in the door of our home, hugging my kids, kissing her, and regaling her with the tale of how the Holy Spirit led me to go into an adult store. Yeah, that would go over like a fart in an elevator. I still wasn't totally convinced I was hearing Holy Spirit, and I was half mad at Him for not helping me protect my mind from this deceptive spirit despite my desperate attempts to resist this devil. But I also had a strange peace in my spirit, like I'd felt so many times before when I had heard Him speak. My intellect was completely confused - this made absolutely no sense - but my spirit was alarmingly at peace and confident that this was right.

I exited and pulled into a gravel parking lot outside the store. I looked around nervously, as if someone I knew from back home in Iowa was going to see me there and report me to my wife and the leaders of the church where I lead worship. At that moment, a woman appeared in the doorway with a small dog on a leash. She let the dog off the leash; a bathroom break for the dog and a smoke break for her. Except once it was off the leash, that sucker took off like a freaking greyhound. I thought for sure it was gone for good. Soon it reappeared from behind the building and zoomed past her, going the opposite direction. This thing was crazy, and it didn't matter how loud the woman yelled its name. It wasn't going back on that leash without a fight, or at least until it got in a good bathroom break and several laps.

FOR 15 MINUTES I DROVE BACK DOWN INTERSTATE 44, FUMING MAD, ARGUING WITH HOLY SPIRIT ABOUT HOW OUT OF BOUNDS IT WAS TO GO INTO AN ADULT SEX NOVELTIES STORE.

I was instantly overjoyed and relieved. Maybe this was a simple assignment from the Holy Spirit to help this woman retrieve her dog? Weird, but, hey, Holy Spirit can say some weird things...

I hopped out of the truck and started hollering the dog's name along with her, which solicited a strange look from her. Eventually the dog, miraculously, came over to me and laid down, panting. I pet his head as she hurried over, put his leash back on, muttered a quick "thank you", and hurried back into the store with her dog in tow.

I stood there in the parking lot, confused about what to do next. I figured my heroic dog recovery would naturally lead to an opportunity to talk to her about Jesus or something redemptive, and I was relieved at the prospect of not having to enter the building. But now what? "Holy Spirit, can I leave now?" Again the answer dropped into my gut, "No, go inside".

I walked down the broken sidewalk leading up to the front door. This place was a dump. I imagined the countless enslaved souls who had walked down this broken path into this landfill of lies and cheap imitation intimacy that promised life, but instead led men into spiritual bondage and relational brokenness. My heart swelled with another feeling as my frustration and confusion gave way to mercy, sorrow, and empathy.

I entered and walked past the check-out desk where the woman was sitting. Without looking up she said, "Look around and let me know if you need anything". My eyes fixed on the floor, trying to guard my peripheral vision, I started wandering down an aisle of DVDs. Holy Spirit! What the hell am I doing here?! I heard Him chuckle in my spirit and His chuckle grew into an all out belly laugh. I thought I was losing my mind. Bewildered, I looked up, and instantly I heard Him say to my spirit.

"You know, I made every body part you see in here. And despite the devil's attempts to pervert it, I love the human body. I made it, I declared it 'good' from day one, and that's still the way it is. Every person represented in these videos and pictures bears my image. Despite the fact that they're completely misrepresenting my intended design for love and intimacy; Satan and his thugs can never change the fact that every human body is a declaration and beautiful representation of Me. You've been delivered from bondage to this false version of intimacy. It holds no power over you any longer. Why do you walk around in here like a terrified orphan? You've been given power over these lies, and your mission today is to deliver a message from me to the woman at the front desk. Remember, there is no place on Earth you can go where I don't have complete dominion and authority, including this store. I'm not threatened by anything in this store, physical or spiritual, and nothing in this store is a threat to you either. I'm here with you. Now go talk to that woman."

A wave of confidence came over me and I picked my head up and stood taller. Finally, I had marching orders, a mission from the King.

Nothing makes you feel ten feet tall and bulletproof more than being handpicked for a special mission by the King of Kings. It was like the Holy Spirit handed me my weapon and steadied my hands and my heart as I put the red dot right on the head of my enemy and I felt a thrill come over me as I prepared to squeeze the trigger.

I walked to the front counter and in a slightly clumsy exchange; I told the woman that I was a Christian and I had been driving down the interstate when I heard the Holy Spirit tell me to stop at this store. I explained I had tried to shrug off the feeling for about 15 miles, but eventually I turned around and came back to the store to speak to her. By this time I assumed Holy Spirit would have given me the word He wanted to share, but He had not. So at the end of my awkward explanation, I simply asked her if there was anything she needed.

The woman's eyes got bigger and swelled with tears as she listened silently to my story. In response to my question, she jumped up and hurried out of the building without a word. I stood there, alone in the store except for a small dog on a leash who looked up at me, still panting from his mid afternoon workout. I heard the Holy Spirit chuckle again and I could sense His reassuring smile; the look of a Father proud because His son had just attempted to do something WAY outside his comfort zone.

I took this as my opportunity and exited the store about ten steps behind the woman. She increased her pace to a jog and covered her mouth, visibly upset. She stopped at the end of the broken sidewalk and as I approached her, I could hear her crying. By this time Holy Spirit had flooded my heart with kindness and compassion, and He just said one word, "Suicide".

My heart broke as I fully realized for the first time that I was on a mission to speak hope over a woman, created in God's image, desperately clinging to life, spiritually drowning in a lie-infested dump, plagued by a spirit of suicide who had been trying to kill her.

With all the kindness and tenderness I had received from Holy Spirit, I simply told her she was valuable. I told her that God saw her today and loved her, and she mattered to Him. I told her she mattered to Him so much that He had grabbed my attention while I was driving by on the interstate, simply to come and give her a blessing from her Heavenly Father to hold on to hope and to receive His love. She cried as I spoke. I asked her name, and I prayed a brief prayer for her to feel the true love and intimacy from Holy Spirit that she was made for. I blessed her mind to be free from any evil influences and prayed for Heaven's richest blessings to flood into her life in tangible ways. There was no altar call, and she didn't recite a prayer to receive Christ, but I know I'd accomplished what Holy Spirit had assigned for me to do, nothing more, nothing less. I finished praying and asked her if she needed money or anything at all. She looked up at me, her mascara streaked down her face as dark black tears dripped off her chin. As she choked back sobs, she simply said, "I just need the strength to make it through one more day. And you gave that to me. Thank you." I gave her a hug, and said, "I didn't give that to you, Holy Spirit gave that to you, because He loves you, and long after I leave, He'll still be here for you." Then I said goodbye, got in my truck and drove away.

I pulled back onto I44 and in peace-filled silence drove on to Oklahoma City. While I drove, I marveled at the depths of our King's goodness and love and was grateful that He would use an ordinary man like me to share His goodness and love with one of His precious daughters that day.

I have felt no calling to turn this into a ministry, nor has this become a routine practice in my travels - much to my wife's relief. I'd never done this sort of thing before this day and have not felt prompted to do it since.

I have no agenda but simply to obey my King - even if it sounds totally insane, and it takes me an extra 30 miles to resolve it. At the end of the day, I'm all in, and the King knows it. I can't go back to the shallows after I've enjoyed such sweet fellowship with Him in deep waters; after I've experienced His heart for me and His crazy compassion for others; after I've had the chance to see Him release prisoners and set captives free. I'm all in for whatever He wants me to do. On that day in the Oklahoma prairie, He wanted to speak hope to a woman at an adult sex store. Tomorrow, who knows... I just know that if He wants to enlist me to do it, I'm all in. To see Him touch people, renew their hope, and revive their spirit is the best thing on Earth. Kings, we GET to be ambassadors of hope and love in a world drowning in despair and hopelessness. Are you all in?

Chapter 17

SPIRITUAL TEFLON

Are you UNoffendable? If so, then, I believe, you will inherit favor and authority by default. If you're easily offended, unforgiving, or hold on to past wounds and nurse grudges, then you won't.

Your ability to remain in peace and exhibit self-control when someone attacks you is a key character trait of kings. The world may perceive this to be weakness, however, as my pastor Kevin has taught us for many years, this is actually the quality of meekness. It's power under control.

> *Matthew 5:38–48 (NLT): 38 "You have heard the law that says the punishment must match the injury: 'An eye for an eye, and a tooth for a tooth.' 39 But I say, do not resist an evil person! If someone slaps you on the right cheek, offer the other cheek also. 40 If you are sued in court and your shirt is taken from you, give your coat, too. 41 If a soldier demands that you carry his gear for a mile, carry it two miles. 42 Give to those who ask, and don't turn away from those who want to borrow. 43 You have heard the law that says, 'Love your neighbor' and hate your enemy. 44 But I say, love your enemies! Pray for those who persecute you! 45 In that way, you will be acting as true children of your Father in heaven.*

For he gives his sunlight to both the evil and the good, and he sends rain on the just and the unjust alike. 46 If you love only those who love you, what reward is there for that? Even corrupt tax collectors do that much. 47 If you are kind only to your friends, how are you different from anyone else? Even pagans do that. 48 But you are to be perfect, even as your Father in heaven is perfect.

Have you ever been slapped? Really, physically, slapped? Perhaps you should be. I think we'd have a much greater sense of what this passage is saying if we had any clue about the level of offense Jesus is talking about here. Most of us get offended when our food takes too long at a restaurant. Let's get real for a minute. Most of us know nothing of the kind of persecution and in-your-face physical, mental, and spiritual abuse Jesus is talking about here.

YOUR ABILITY TO REMAIN IN PEACE AND EXHIBIT SELF-CONTROL WHEN SOMEONE ATTACKS YOU IS A KEY CHARACTER TRAIT OF KINGS.

So why would Jesus say to just take it? Not only that, but to go the extra mile and welcome it, and love and pray for our abusers?

That's easy. It's to keep us free. There is a demon whose name is Offense. He hates you, and like all the other demons we've talked about, he wants to imprison you, steal your destiny, your joy, your physical health, and ultimately, take your life. He partners with your old nature and entices you to retaliate when you're offended. Because this makes sense at an Earthly, legal, level, it can be difficult to detect when he's influencing you as you consider what is just and fair in these situations.

When somebody does us wrong, there should be a simple formula for resolving the injustice, right? If someone steals, the resolution is to return what was stolen. But the spirit of Offense is constantly goading us to judgment and anger, to carry around a bitter grudge against our offender, whether or not the injustice is made right. His thoughts sound something like this... "I'll never forgive them. They don't deserve it. Why me God?"

The process starts off innocently enough with what seems like just an honest inventory of the situation itself, but if we don't recognize the trap, it can spiral into a full-blown abduction of our mind. Before we realize it, we wind up in a mental prison of judgment, criticism, anger, bitterness, jealousy, depression and worse.

Jesus knows this, and in His wisdom, He's given us the ultimate weapon against Offense. It's called forgiveness and blessing. The reality is that we don't extend forgiveness for the sake of our offender, or because they've given us a good apology, made things right, or seem remorseful. We forgive for our sake and to remain free. Unforgiveness and offense are toxins that poison our life. When we forgive, we're not excusing our offender's behavior, we're simply expelling the poison from our lives.

In my experience, this demon is persistent, constantly reminding me of past wrongs and wounds inflicted by others like a worn out recording on repeat in my mind. He also works in conjunction with other demons that attack by flooding my mind with other lies and negative thoughts during times of fatigue, trial, and persecution. He waits for opportune moments to attack, when all hope is lost, the moment you hear the bad news, the day your car breaks down, you lose your job; you get the divorce papers, your business partner betrays you and then here he comes.

The attack can be very effective because in those moments we are weakened by circumstances and the arguments he presents sound SO appealing to our old nature and our intellectual mind. When all hell is breaking loose in your life, it is quite easy to take a quick inventory of the situations and quickly partner with negative thoughts and emotions, right?

Jesus would rather have us avoid this trap altogether because, through His incredible sacrifice, we are free. No, I mean REALLY free.

Free to respond to people and circumstances around us as though we belong to a different realm and are not bound to the normal human reactions and emotions we experience here on Earth. We are alive in Christ and dead to sin, and therefore, sin has no power to dictate our actions without our permission. It can be very persuasive, but ultimately we have the final say, and when offended, we can respond with grace. When we are cursed, we can return a blessing. This is not only possible, it is NORMAL behavior for kings in the Kingdom. Our new nature is to forgive, respond with powerful self-control, and react with love because the Holy Spirit lives inside us. The demons that entice us to retaliate, to get revenge, or to harbor a grudge don't have control over us, unless we give it to them by agreeing with their arguments and believing their lies.

One of the most freeing moments of my life came when I realized for the first time that I didn't have to be offended, ever. I can listen to a politician I strongly disagree with and not be offended. I can get cut off in traffic and not be offended. I can get fired, lose my house, have my ideas stolen, be rejected by my peers, be verbally attacked by someone close to me, and not be offended. I can function without keeping score, without settling the debts, and without getting justice for myself.

Kings, not only can we do this, but if we want to avoid partnership with demonic mindsets that will rob us of our joy, peace, and destiny, then we MUST do this. I'd like to suggest that remaining in peace, and resisting the demon of offense, is one of the primary ways you maintain your mental health, spiritual freedom, and access to your authority and favor in the Kingdom.

Take king David as an example. He inherited the throne, not through seeking justice for the offenses committed against him by Saul - even though he would have been totally justified in doing so by Earth's standards of justice. David was the anointed king, but resisted the urge on two separate occasions to kill Saul and seize His throne, despite the urging of his Mighty Men. Human wisdom told him to seize his opportunity to rule and reign. After all, Saul was arguably a terrible king, and David had been anointed for the role and position by Samuel. But he restrained himself and God GAVE the throne to him because he would not give into the spirit of offense or take matters into his own hands, but instead, he served and honored Saul, a crazy, tormented king. Hmmm.... lots of lessons there, to be sure.

Jesus' command here isn't some test that only super-spiritual Christians can pass in order to be accepted and approved by God. It's a primary key to accessing the abundant life He promised and walking in the power and authority of Holy Spirit. You get to decide. You can forgive your offenders, turn the other cheek, and move on with your inheritance and your heart intact. Or you can wallow in self-pity as you ruminate on the injustices of your life and crucify the villain a thousand times in your mind. If you choose the latter, you'll end up sidelined in your own life, wasting away in a self-imposed prison of anger and depression. Don't do it.

YOU CAN FORGIVE YOUR OFFENDERS, TURN THE OTHER CHEEK, AND MOVE ON WITH YOUR INHERITANCE AND YOUR HEART INTACT.

King's I know how hard this is. I've been there, done that, took a lot of prayer to get free and delivered. It's a cunning trap that has ensnared a lot of kings, causing them to be taken out of their places of authority and destiny. But before you think Jesus is soft on justice and the law, let's look at another Scripture where he supports the Mosaic law wholeheartedly.

> *Matthew 5:17–18 (NLT): 17 "Don't misunderstand why I have come. I did not come to abolish the law of Moses or the writings of the prophets. No, I came to accomplish their purpose. 18 I tell you the truth, until heaven and earth disappear, not even the smallest detail of God's law will disappear until its purpose is achieved.*

So which is it, Jesus, judgment and justice or mercy and forgiveness??? The answer is both. The question is not whether evil will get avenged, it's about who's metering out the justice. Consider Paul's advice below.

> *Romans 12:19–21 (NLT): 19 Dear friends, never take revenge. Leave that to the righteous anger of God. For the Scriptures say,*
>
> *"I will take revenge;*
> *I will pay them back,"*
> *says the Lord.*
>
> *20 Instead,*
> *"If your enemies are hungry, feed them.*
> *If they are thirsty, give them something to drink.*
> *In doing this, you will heap*
> *burning coals of shame on their heads."*
> *21 Don't let evil conquer you, but conquer evil by doing good.*

Righteous justice has to be administered by the correct authority and righteous judgments by the right judge. Last time I looked, that wasn't me.

Jesus has a LOT to say about judging others, and I'd suggest that whenever we allow the demon of offense to influence our thinking, then we've disqualified ourselves from acting as the judge who can dispassionately administer justice to our enemy. Leave that to God. He will make it right. And remember, we are not battling flesh and blood, anyway. So if you seek retribution, seek it from your spiritual foe, not the human puppet or tormented soul he used to attack you.

Kings, this is a nonnegotiable element of your character that Holy Spirit is forging in you right now. The takeaways are many and if you understand that the purpose of the offense is to grow your character in this specific way, then you can partner with the process. This will be tested in your life, probably on an ongoing basis, until you die. If you can get used to turning the other cheek, then you'll get used to walking in more authority and greater freedom. If you seek an "eye for an eye", then you'll probably leave a wake of poor judgments and relational carnage behind you as you slog through life.

There is a jaw-dropping moment in scripture when this truth was driven home for me. But I think it can get lost in the story because it's a brief passage sandwiched in the middle of the most intense circumstance recorded in scripture. But when you catch it, you see that Jesus himself was tempted by this demon at the most critical and opportune moment of His life.

As Jesus was hanging on the cross, having been recently betrayed by one of His disciples, falsely accused by the religious authorities, mocked, spit on, beaten, and whipped to near death by soldiers, abandoned by ALL of His closest friends, about to breathe His last breath, He said one of the most profound things to come out of any human's mouth. This wasn't a final teaching moment that He spoke for the benefit of His disciples and onlookers. This was an incredible demonstration of self-control and kindness to those who had hung Him there to die. This was Jesus practicing what He preached in Matthew 5.

Rather than calling down a legion of angels to stomp humankind into a puddle, and rather than cursing everyone around Him and demanding justice, He blesses His killers. Recall His words to the Father as He was bleeding out....

> *Luke 23:34 (NLT): 34 Jesus said, "Father, forgive them, for they don't know what they are doing."*

They weren't asking for forgiveness at that moment, nor were they showing any remorse whatsoever. As the ultimate violators of justice and offenders of all things humane and dignified, *they* definitely didn't deserve His forgiveness. The voice of Offense must have been screaming in His ear at that moment. How wonderful that Holy Spirit's voice was even louder. In that moment, Jesus shows us, by example, how to release the toxin of unforgiveness and how to smash the head of Offense. Within the next 72 hours, He would inherit all authority in heaven, on earth, and under the earth, even authority over death itself.

Kings, this is a tough one, but I trust you know what to do. Forgiveness is a gift for you, and a weapon for you to use on your REAL enemy. So do it. Get the demon of offense in your crosshairs and pull the trigger, and don't look back. When he tries to come back, kill him again by lavishing forgiveness on those who've hurt you.

Holy Spirit, I release the grace for this mission over my brothers today. I pray for these kings, my brothers, co-heirs with Christ, and faithful ambassadors of the King of Heaven's Armies to receive a radical impartation of wisdom, grace, and forgiveness so that they can walk in true freedom and power in every area of their life. I rebuke the lies and revoke the authority of the spirit of offense over their lives, their families, and over their churches, in Jesus' name. I declare the dawning of a new season that the kings of God are revealed to the Earth not by our arguments and rants against those who have offended us, but by the power and presence of our King of Kings showed through unconditional love and forgiveness, in Jesus' name, Amen!

Chapter 18

"DO YOU WANT TO GET WELL?" "I CAN'T BECAUSE ____________"

In John 5, Jesus approaches a lame man who has been ill for 38 years. 38 years!!! He and many others like him spent their days in and around one particular gate in Jerusalem known as the Sheep gate and at a nearby pool called Bethesda. It was said that an angel would periodically come down and stir the waters in the pool and if you could get into the waters at that time, you would be healed. I love this passage because it's an honest conversation between Jesus and a person who needs a miracle. I'm stunned at how much this conversation sounds similar to conversations I have had with Jesus and how much I can learn from Jesus' demonstration of Kingship here.

A few immediate observations and takeaways... First of all, we're talking about Jesus. He doesn't ask questions for information. He already knows the answers before we answer and knows what He's going to do. His questions are designed to reveal things to us, not to Him.

Second, if/when Jesus asks you a question; don't answer a different question. Jesus specifically asks a simple, pointed question. Do you want to be healed? Lots of commentators have speculated about the motivation of the question, what it meant, and how it would have come across to the crippled man. In my opinion, it was probably insulting to the man. Imagine being asked this question after being lame for 38 years! If I'd been lame for 38 years, and some "Christian" walked up to me and asked me the question, "do you want to be healed", I'd be offended. But that's just me. I'd probably also be grateful that someone bothered to talk to me and asked me anything at all.

I think it is interesting that the man answered a totally different question than the one Jesus asks. Again, I see similarities between this crippled man and myself. Jesus asks a Yes/No question. The response from the man is an explanation of WHY he can't get healed. Jesus didn't ask him, "Why can't you get healed?"

I believe the man's response revealed a mindset that had been ingrained in his thinking for 38 years that went something like this...

> *"... the pool bubbles, we all try to get in, the first one or two in get healed, the rest of us wait till next year."*

Perhaps after the first few attempts, he thought, *"maybe I'll ask someone to help me next year"*. But after a few attempts, and no help, he resigns himself to the reality of his situation. He's taken inventory of the situation, knows the facts, has "run the numbers" and healing isn't on the menu for him, and he can recite all the reasons why.

So in order to inoculate himself from deep discouragement and disappointment, he makes peace with his lot in life and commiserates by the pool with the others like him where they live out their miserable, afflicted days...one after another.

Jesus confronts his foregone conclusions about his life head on with one question, and then further confounds his presumptions about his life by healing him instantly on the spot. No pool, no bubbles, no help from another person, no pushing and shoving to get in first. Everything this man thought about the healing process was bypassed in an instant and all his 38-year-old paradigms were turned upside down. Healing in his mind was a complicated puzzle he couldn't solve. Jesus destroys the formula and introduces a completely new alternative method.

So many times I've heard Holy Spirit say, "Hey! Do you want to do this?" And way too often my response is, "But Lord, I can't because we don't have the money, or the time, or the skills, or the passion, or the team, etc."

I forget He is not actually asking me for my laundry list of reasons I *can't* do something. He is asking me a yes/no question. If I could get beyond past disappointments, past failures, shame, frustration, lack, fear, and a host of other gatekeepers, perhaps I could more easily step into my destiny and enjoy a mindset like He has. See, in His mind, He's God. He's not insecure about His power or position and He can do anything because He's been given all authority. So when He asks if I want to do something with Him, my auto-responder should be "YES!", not the standard litany of excuses why I can't.

Yeah, but what about the 38 years you spent praying, hoping, wishing, dreaming, and NEVER getting healed? My answer is, I don't know. I realize that many of us live in the tension of prayers, petitions, dreams and prophecies yet to be fulfilled. I know that for some of us, our hearts have grown cold in the waiting. I can see it in some of your eyes and hear it in your voices as I talk to you about your journey with God. I hear pain and discouragement and in the same way I battle the disappointments of my own unanswered petitions.

Let's pivot to discussing disappointment and enduring trials for a minute...

Honestly, if there is no REAL access to peace and joy for Sons of God while they patiently endure trials and wait for breakthrough, then this Gospel that we believe has been totally misrepresented by Jesus, and by scripture. If that's the case, then what else has been misrepresented? Heaven? Eternal life? Let's be honest, if peace that passes understanding isn't a real thing, then perhaps eternal life is also not a thing. If we can't trust that it's ALL true, then it isn't worth the energy, time, money, and passion we pour out for it.

If the "good news" of the Gospel isn't, as Graham Cooke says, "such good news that it borders on fantasy", then, honestly, I'm out. I've got better things to spend my life on, and so do you.

But here's what I believe. Even Jesus Himself endured the cross for the JOY set before Him. That means that while He was enduring the cross, He was focused on the joy that was coming - a future payday that included you and me, coming into a fully restored relationship with Him. A day when He would ride victoriously into Heaven with the keys to Hell. A day when His Father would exalt Him with ALL authority in Heaven, on Earth, and under the Earth, in this age, and in the age to come. Do you know how to access THAT kind of joy? Joy that would make the cross, the pain, the abuse, the humiliation, and the eventual death worth it all?

Kings, when you get a revelation of a process modeled by Jesus, it needs to become a priority to understand and model the same behavior. Our wholehearted pursuit and discovery of deep, deep intimacy with Holy Spirit has been modeled by our older big brother, Jesus, when on numerous occasions, He went away to pray with His Father. He knew Holy Spirit to such a degree that He could endure negative circumstances because of His magnificent presence. Many of our brothers in the Bible had similar encounters with the Lord that empowered them as well. For example, Moses' glowing face, Daniel's lion-taming experience, Paul and Silas's worship concert that brought down the jail cell walls, Stephen's visions of God during his stoning, and so many others.

If you've endured protracted seasons of loss or hardship, be encouraged. David was anointed king and then spent the next 17 years herding sheep, living in caves, hiding in enemy cities, working for enemy kings and dodging spears from Saul, the king he knew he would one day replace.

Joseph, after receiving a prophetic vision of his future where his brothers and parents all bowed down and worshipped him, spent several years in a variety of tight spots, including a pit, slavery, and jail, all unjustified and unwarranted.

Paul endured a thorn in his flesh and kept on traveling and ministering to others, despite being beaten, imprisoned, and shipwrecked.

I could go on, but you get the point. We don't like this part of life, but the sooner we make peace with it, the sooner the fear surrounding it will leave you. You may have already spent 38 years waiting for your healing but the real question is can you remain connected to hope in the waiting, and when Jesus shows up can you silence disappointment, discouragement and embrace Him, your savior and deliverer who has finally come?

Your advancement in the kingdom, as a king, is predicated on your heart's connection with Holy Spirit and that connection will be tested by fire. Whether it's the fire of trial, or the fire of promotion, poverty or wealth, cave or the palace - it all will test your connection with Holy Spirit. The psalmist asks, "who can ascend the mountain of God?" and then answers his own question, "one with a pure heart and clean hands".

How do you get a pure heart? Same way you purify anything, heat, sifting, fire, scrubbing, washing, refining, etc.

The way I rely on money instead of God, for example, is an impurity in my heart that will not serve me well in my next promotion into wealth or influence. God knows just how embedded this impurity is in my heart. But here's the problem, I don't. I wholeheartedly believe that I'm relying on God. Just ask me! But suddenly a different "me" shows up when the bank account runs dry and the pantry is bare. God can see that there are unrefined impurities that I cannot see, and that's the point. He's faithful and true, to forgive us our sins and cleanse us from all unrighteousness. I like the forgiveness part, not a big fan of the cleansing part.

A king has to be trustworthy and steadfast in their conviction and beliefs - not double minded. Otherwise, you'll quit in the heat of battle. You won't stand and defeat a giant. You'll run. You will compromise on core values when you should hold your ground and you'll end up a defeated, impotent king negotiating with your enemies for your life.

When you endure trials, hardships, and challenges for a long time, you develop a trust and confidence in God that can only be forged in that kind of fiery season. Seasons of plenty and ease are not super helpful for driving us into greater intimacy with God or building faith. They do other things, but not that. And let's be honest, if we seek deliverance in the midst of it, aren't we short-cutting the process? When we circumvent the refinement process, the end product is not pure. If we tell God to turn down the furnace, what we're really telling Him is that we want our impurities and junk MORE than want the abundant life He's set before us because getting rid of our junk is too painful, costs us too much, or isn't worth it. Believe me, I know this tension is VERY real. I couldn't begin to count the number of times I've wanted to quit. I can't tell you how many nights I've cried out to God to take me, to relieve the pain. I've whined and accused Him of not caring. I've cursed Him during hard seasons of life because He seemed like a harsh bully, or worse, totally absent. When I lost my job, when our marriage nearly ended, when we were on the brink of bankruptcy, etc. Perhaps my fellow kings know what I'm talking about?

WHEN YOU BECAME A KING, YOU VOLUNTARILY SMASHED YOUR EXCUSE MACHINE.

The cave prepares you to rule and reign with dignity, honor, and wisdom once you're in the castle. It makes you able to empathize with people who hurt in a way that is authentic. I wish it wasn't so, but it is. And like Jesus, if you can fix your eyes on the joy set before you - the payday, intimacy with Him, confidence, strength, authority, favor, promotion - then you can endure and do anything - just like Jesus.

James 1:2–8 (NLT)

2 Dear brothers and sisters, when troubles of any kind come your way, consider it an opportunity for great joy. 3 For you know that when your faith is tested, your endurance has a chance to grow. 4 So let it grow, for when your endurance is fully developed, you will be perfect and complete, needing nothing. 5 If you need wisdom, ask our generous God, and he will give it to you. He will not rebuke you for asking. 6 But when you ask him, be sure that your faith is in God alone. Do not waver, for a person with divided loyalty is as unsettled as a wave of the sea that is blown and tossed by the wind. 7 Such people should not expect to receive anything from the Lord. 8 Their loyalty is divided between God and the world, and they are unstable in everything they do.

Matthew 5:11–12 (NLT): 11 "God blesses you when people mock you and persecute you and lie about you and say all sorts of evil things against you because you are my followers. 12 Be happy about it! Be very glad! For a great reward awaits you in heaven. And remember, the ancient prophets were persecuted in the same way.

When you became a king, you voluntarily smashed your excuse machine. When Jesus shows up and extends a personal invitation into your destiny, your healing, your breakthrough, kings don't respond with excuses based on their experiences. They hearken to the sound of their King's voice, and their hearts surge with hope, as they align with Holy Spirit's power, and purpose.

Kings, perhaps it's time to renew a commitment to pray for something you gave up on many years ago. Perhaps it's time to evict discouragement and disappointment from your life and stop commiserating with others around you over losses, tragedies, and unresolved circumstances. You're a king with the privilege of crushing your enemies with the joy of your King which is your strength, and peace that passes understanding. This is your rightful place on the Earth. So I have just one question. Do you want to get well?

CONCLUSION

Kings, there is so much more I feel like Holy Spirit has to say to us as we walk this road of kingship together. These chapters are just the humble beginnings of what I know will be a deep awakening to His goodness and an ongoing exploration of the vast Kingdom that awaits us as we learn to walk in our full authority and inheritance. Revelation from Heaven is our currency along the path. Holy Spirit is our guide who gives wisdom and strength generously so that we can successfully navigate the challenges and enemies we'll face along the way.

I hope that you've been inspired by the endless possibilities waiting for you in the Kingdom. I hope you've gained a burning desire to seek ageless wisdom to answer the questions I asked when we began this journey together.

> *"What if...?".*
>
> *What if there is a place of such intense peace and joy reserved for me in relationship with Holy Spirit that my outer life could be an authentic reflection of my inner reality and not just an act?*
>
> *What if I can calm storms and kill giants in my life, and teach my wife, children, and grandchildren to do the same?*

What if I could change the atmosphere in the room from despair to hope just by showing up because Holy Spirit's presence in me is tangible?

What if the approval and affirmation of people had no power over me, but instead, I was free to pursue my divine assignment without hesitation or reservation?

What if instead of insulating my life from pain out of fear, I could learn to love the fire of refinement and view every trial as a stepping stone into a promotion of authority, wisdom, strength, and intimacy with Holy Spirit?

What if the supernatural was just my "natural" state?

What if I could generously administer the resources of Heaven into my family relationships, my business, city, church, school, and every other area of my life?

Could this be real? Isn't this what Jesus achieved for us when He died, rose from the dead, and was seated in heaven with all authority, dominion, and power?

Kings, as I stated at the beginning, I'm "all in '' to discover this new life and walk in my divine destiny as a humble servant of the King of Kings, who has given us the keys to heaven and Earth, and I pray that you are too.

When Jesus left His disciples on Earth, He gave them His final marching orders, which we know as "The Great Commission". We are blessed to have a couple different Gospel writers' accounts, Matthew and Mark's.

Matthew 28:16–20 (NLT): Then the eleven disciples left for Galilee, going to the mountain where Jesus had told them to go. 17 When they saw him, they worshiped him—but some of them doubted! 18 Jesus came and told his disciples, "I have been given all authority in heaven and on earth. 19 Therefore, go and make disciples of all the nations, baptizing them in the name of the Father and the Son and the Holy Spirit. 20 Teach these new disciples to obey all the commands I have given you. And be sure of this: I am with you always, even to the end of the age."

Mark 16:15–18 (NLT): And then he told them, "Go into all the world and preach the Good News to everyone. 16 Anyone who believes and is baptized will be saved. But anyone who refuses to believe will be condemned. 17 These miraculous signs will accompany those who believe: They will cast out demons in my name, and they will speak in new languages. 18 They will be able to handle snakes with safety, and if they drink anything poisonous, it won't hurt them. They will be able to place their hands on the sick, and they will be healed."

My brothers, these are the same words Jesus speaks to us right up to this very hour. The charge has never changed. Whether you've lost sight of His vision for your life in the past is not relevant anymore. You're here now, and your invitation back into the fight, back into mission, and into your destiny is waiting for you.

Regardless of what lies ahead, all authority has been given to our King, and He has entrusted it to us, His friends, His brothers, His kings for one purpose: To enforce His agenda on Earth, to make Him famous, to establish the supremacy of our King and His Kingdom, to model His goodness and glory as we make disciples and set captives free.

My father-in-law's favorite movie is It's a Wonderful Life. Like George Bailey, he is a banker in the small Midwest town where we're from. Like George Bailey, his life has blessed scores of people in the town, his employees at the bank, individual citizens, families, local businesses, schools, and churches, just to name a few. I often imagine what might have happened to our town if he, and others like him, had taken an easier path, to not step fully into their destiny, to not lead boldly, give generously, and serve well in the assignment our King gave them. Like in the movie, I fear our small community would have lost many battles, perhaps even lost its soul. How many "Pottersvilles" exist because God's kings have neglected their assignment, abandoned their post, and allowed evil to reign? But not my father-in-law. He gets up every day, goes into work, and serves the King of Kings, like a king, and holds the line against the evil schemes of the enemy. He is an ambassador of the goodness and faithfulness of God, on display day after day, for the world to see.

My father also has a favorite movie, Hidalgo. He loves the underdog story, the epic three thousand mile race across the Arabian desert filled with peril for Frank Hopkins, legendary endurance horse racer, and his wild American mustang, Hidalgo. Frank's famous line from the movie, which has become a favorite of my Dad's, is "Let'er buck!", which Frank says to Hidalgo when it's time to race. Indeed, that motto fits my dad's personality perfectly. I wonder, where would I be if I'd never seen a fearless risk-taker go after something, even against the odds? Where would I be if I'd never had the chance to learn from this master craftsman, filled with ideas, visions, machines and solutions that continue to leave a Kingdom impact on industries, businesses, and people worldwide? He is a craftsman, a gift to Earth, carrying Kingdom vision and creativity. And whether he's gearing up for a coast-to-coast oversized load in his 18-wheeler or putting on his welding apron, he's putting on the royal garments that our King made just for him.

I'm grateful for these kings in my life, and so many others, who've demonstrated the true nature of the Kingdom by faithfully executing their assignments and living their lives fully surrendered to the King of Kings. What a gift.

Tomorrow you'll probably wake up in your bed, in your city, and prepare to go to your job. But never forget this reality: you are first and foremost a citizen of Heaven and you will be long after this Earth passes away. As a member of God's royal family, your mission is to be the walking embodiment of the glory of Heaven. You are meant to shine, to show off the King's nature, the greatness of His creativity, generosity, power, kindness, and love. Your life is designed to cause those around you to marvel, to wonder, to ask questions, to reveal a better way into a superior reality. It is our pleasure to be ambassadors for a Kingdom that flows with all the power, resources, and strategies that the Earth longs to see and experience. We get to be the ones that cast out the devil and his demons, to release those who have been enslaved by him and to welcome them into the family of God.

You have one life. One shot to leave a Heavenly mark on Earth that will resonate for all eternity; one chance to take your seat among the great cloud of witnesses that have been cheering us on for centuries. The Kingdom is a matter of growing Redwoods, not roses. We are part of a great family of heroes who've labored before us and who cheer us on to this very hour. By God's grace we will have the joy of commissioning the next generation in the same way Jesus commissioned his disciples; to do greater things than we did, to search out new territory, unlock new secrets of the Kingdom, and discover endless treasures prepared for them by our King. This is the legacy of a true king.

The Earth is groaning, waiting eagerly, expectantly, watching for us to emerge with divine purpose, wisdom, strategic solutions, and unquenchable zeal born from an intimate connection to another realm. Kings, this is our mission, and this is the hour we were born to shine brightest. Holy Spirit beckons us into a lifelong adventure; the deepest, most meaningful life we could possibly imagine. Brothers, I'm all in. And would love to run with you. Are you all in?

ACKNOWLEDGMENTS

I saved my best writing for this section because it is the most important part of this book, for without the people I'm about to thank there would be no book.

First, to Lexi, my new friend who has helped me navigate this process for the first time. I swear, you're are the most "on it" person I've ever worked with. If I had ten of you, I think we could conquer a small country! I so appreciate your hard work and guidance to bring this from a humble and simple document into a "real" book.

Second, to the mighty men, the kings, my brothers and sisters in arms, the hungry and the humble that I've had the privilege of running with over the past two decades and right up to this very moment. Your zeal for our King and His Kingdom have inspired me more than you could possibly know and I'm forever changed because of the things I've learned in your presence. I'd gladly go into battle with any one of you because I know at the end of the day, you lean not on your own understanding, but acknowledge our King above all others, even if you look foolish, even if it appears counterintuitive, even if it costs you. You are trustworthy kings, tested by both abundance and lack, water and fire, who can carry the weight of Kingdom glory so well. I eagerly anticipate the next coffee, scotch, or glass of wine we will inevitably share. You are the glorious "nobodies" the Earth is longing for and I can't wait to continue to watch as the Kingdom manifests in the words you speak, the books you write, and at the diligent and faithful work of your hands. Our future together is so bright, so lit, and our King has such incredible faith in us. It's time for us to ignite.

Third, to my mother and father, and my mother-in-law and father-in-law. You've put up with a lot! The tender (and at times not so tender) guidance, patience, and steadfast love you've shown me is in itself a tangible manifestation of the goodness of the Kingdom in my life. You've watched for years as I've wrestled through my own ideas about the King, church, my failures, and successes, and everything in between. Your example of loyalty and love is a legacy I cherish and hope to pass on even more to my own children as they emerge into kings and queens.

Next, to my children, Ava, Wyatt, Isabelle, Layla, and Ryder; you've watched me struggle, process, and worship my way through a lot over the past 10 years. I love with a fierce and consuming love and I so appreciate the maturity you've all shown - well beyond your years. I love how you've asked great questions, and processed Kingdom life at a level most adults can't fathom. You are all kings and queens and the Earth is lucky to have you coming onto the scene, for you carry the Kingdom in your bones, and the unquenchable love of God in your hearts. You are world changers and my ceiling is your floor. Point me in the direction of your dreams and together with Heaven, we'll make it happen, for the glory of our King.

Lastly, to my unbelievable wife, the absolute love of my life, who captured my heart over 25 years ago. I am so glad I wrecked that waverunner just to get your attention. You've been the absolute rock and quintessential Proverbs 31 woman. I could write an entire book on the amazing ways you've demonstrated what it really means to be a queen, beloved by the Father and always ready to surrender your agenda to His, no matter the cost. I'm in awe of how much you've grown in grace, beauty, and power over the course of our life together and I'm your champion to the end. You've probably listened to me preach the most of anyone, and even when I was struggling, floundering, and causing you pain, you still remained, you abided, and you never even considered walking away. The passion and love I feel for you is stronger and more vibrant than ever and I'm so excited to see what our next adventure holds. Wherever it leads, I'll be holding your hand as we go.

WHERE TO CONNECT

For more information about A King's Fire ministry, connecting with like-minded kings, speaking engagements, and consulting with Matt Hugg, please visit:

AKINGSFIRE.COM

Made in the USA
Monee, IL
21 December 2021

e4a595d2-dbdd-44d5-ad01-bf6be9e5711cR01